NONFICTION BOOKS BY CORK MILLNER

Vintage Valley

Sherry—The Golden Wine of Spain

Wines and Wineries of Santa Barbara

Recipes by the Winemakers

Santa Barbara Celebrities—Conversations from the American Riviera

The Art of Interviewing

Write from the Start

COAUTHORED WITH LYNDA MILLNER

Looking Great *Without* Diet or Exercise

COAUTHORED WITH CASS WARNER SPERLING

Hollywood Be Thy Name

COAUTHORED WITH STAN LOVE

Who Loves Brian?

COAUTHORED WITH HARA

Flamingo! *An African Odyssey*

A FIRESIDE BOOK

PUBLISHED BY SIMON & SCHUSTER

NEW YORK

LONDON

TORONTO

SYDNEY

TOKYO

SINGAPORE

Write

FROM THE START

Cork Millner

FIRESIDE
Simon & Schuster Building
Rockefeller Center
1230 Avenue of the Americas
New York, New York 10020

FIRESIDE and colophon are registered trademarks
of Simon and Schuster Inc.

Designed by Liney Li
Manufactured in the United States of America

1   3   5   7   9   10   8   6   4   2

Library of Congress Cataloging in Publication Data
Millner, Cork, date
Write from the start / Cork Millner
p.   cm.
Includes bibliographical references and index.
1. Authorship.   I. Title.
PN145.M488   1992
808'.02—dc20   91-42804
CIP

ISBN: 0-671-72442-8

Editorial guidelines on pp. 197–201
used by permission of Sky magazine.

Write from the Start
is dedicated to Barnaby Conrad
and the workshop leaders of the
Santa Barbara Writers Conference.

C O N T E N T S

Introduction: How You Can Become a Selling Writer

"Get black on white."

—Guy de Maupassant

She sat listening intently in the front row of my nonfiction writing class, a pleasant smile on her face. For several weeks she hadn't turned in any of the weekly assignments. She just listened—and smiled.

After the fourth class she came to my desk. "I'm a licensed therapist," she began. "I counsel wives of alcoholic husbands. I'd like to write a magazine article about my work."

We talked about her idea, how to organize it, and I suggested she include case histories of women she had counseled.

The next week she turned in the first draft of the article. It was well written, with a balanced blend of narrative, anecdotes, character, dialogue and problem-solving concepts.

"This may sound silly," she said, pausing, "but I have enough material for a book. Should I write it? I even have a title."

"What do you want to call it?" I asked.

"Women Who Love Too Much."

Robin Norwood wrote her book and it became a smash bestseller, propelling her to national fame and fortune.

How did Robin Norwood succeed when so many other writers fail? Quite simply, if you want to become a published writer, you must *learn* the profession of writing. Like Robin Norwood.

Who is this book written for? Every writer who wants to break into print!

Virtually every literate person believes he has at least one story in him that an editor wants. Many of them have tried a little writing; they think their dabblings would be saleable if only they knew how to fix them up and sell them. These writers include:

- Grandma, who has written an article about her needlecraft she knows is just right for *Early American Life*.
- Junior, who wants to publish his Eagle Scout experiences in *Boy's Life*.
- Baby boomers, who are now at the point in their lives where they either have something to say or want professional visibility and recognition through writing. They want to share their knowledge and business acumen with readers of *Success*, *Business Today* and *Ink* magazine.
- Retired folks, who have an experience they want to share with the readers of *Modern Maturity*.
- Anyone who wants to write something publishable for his or her hometown newspaper, church gazette or club newsletter.

Unfortunately, most of these would-be writers don't have a clue how to go about writing and selling their manuscripts.

James Michener once said, "Many people who want to be

writers don't really want to be writers. They want to *have been* writers. They wish they had a book in print."

Michener is right. Too many people fantasize about writing without ever putting pen to paper. They dream of success rather than setting goals and working to achieve that success.

Let's face it, any literate person can write. There are untold thousands of people walking the streets of America who have a chance to break into print. The question is: Why don't more of these potential wordsmiths become selling writers? The answer is simple: *They don't take the time to learn how to be writers.*

Sure, everybody does a little bit of writing: letters home, business correspondence, memos, club or church newsletters. But doing a little bit of writing is about the same as doing a little bit of exercise. You don't build your body's muscles with occasional exercise and you don't build your literary muscles by writing shopping lists.

Look at it this way: If you were any attorney, wouldn't you read stacks of books about law? If you were an airline pilot, wouldn't you study your flight manuals until you knew each emergency procedure by heart? If you don't commit yourself to learning the writer's craft with the same energy you would devote to preparing for any other profession, then it's no wonder you haven't been published.

From this moment on call yourself a writer. When you write or speak to anyone, especially an editor, present yourself as a writer. Not a fledgling writer, not an aspiring writer. A real writer.

Now that you have established that you are a writer, what steps must you take to become a selling writer? What is a *surefire way* to create saleable nonfiction? *Write from the Start* provides the answers. It gives you a detailed, *proven*, step-by-step method for writing and selling magazine articles and nonfiction books. The book's twelve chapters take you, the writer, through the following twelve steps, each programmed to help you break into print.

Surefire Step #1:
Developing Successful Writing Habits

The writer must generate *self-discipline;* write each day; *persevere* when those form rejection slips keep showing up in the mail box; and finally, attack life with a burning *desire* to succeed. Chapter 1 shows you how to begin the process of unleashing your creativity by harnessing and channeling your energies.

Surefire Step #2:
Encouraging the Creative Impulse

Albert Einstein developed the theory of relativity by visualizing himself standing on a ray of light. Vincent van Gogh spoke of "pictures coming to me as in a dream." To end writer's block and open your window of creativity, Chapter 2 shows you how to get those first words on paper and then use such inspirational methods as right-brain writing and stream-of-consciousness writing to keep those words flowing.

Surefire Step #3:
Learning Basic Writing Techniques

As a writer, you need to understand the forces of imagery—sight, smell, taste, touch, and hearing—to create scenes the reader can *see*. Chapter 3 shows you how to enhance your writing style to compel an editor to read your manuscript; how to develop your research skills to make your writing creditable; and how to develop your rewriting skills to make it perfect.

Surefire Step #4:
Developing an Idea Factory

Mark Twain said, "Adam was the only man who, when he said a good thing, knew that nobody had said it before him."

What sells nonfiction? *Ideas*. Not necessarily new ideas; more often old ideas with a new slant, a new focus.

Where does a new writer find ideas that will entice editors? That old adage, "Write what you know," holds true today. Ideas come from personal experience, knowledge, interest and what you read in magazines and newspapers. Chapter 4 shows you how to develop an idea factory that will continually produce marketable ideas.

Surefire Step #5:
Writing Great Leads

As I stepped into the bathtub with a glass of champagne and my best friend's husband, the doorbell rang.

Hooked? You bet! So is the editor. The article's lead is the most important paragraph you can write. Chapter 5 teaches lead-writing techniques that grab the reader's attention fast—and hold it.

Surefire Step #6:
Adding Variety to Your Writing

Like a juggler, the competent writer needs to balance anecdotes, quotes, character, action and dialogue to keep the reader turning pages. Chapter 6 shows you how to sustain your reader's interest throughout your article or book chapter.

Surefire Step #7:
Using Fiction Techniques

Chapter 7 shows you how to use such fiction techniques as character development, dialogue and story-telling skills to involve the reader in the action or emotion of a story and to inject life and sparkle into an otherwise prosaic nonfiction piece.

Surefire Step #8:
Mastering the Q's and A's of Interviewing

Getting firsthand, expert quotes will beef up *any* nonfiction work and make it more saleable. Chapter 8 shows how to use the interviewing process to add vitality and credibility to your story. It also demonstrates how to write one of the bestselling types of nonfiction—the personality profile.

Surefire Step #9:
Using Titles That Tantalize

All I Really Need to Know I Learned in Kindergarten, Real Men Don't Eat Quiche, Thin Thighs in 30 Days, The One-Minute Manager: all are bestsellers. Why? The title plays an important part in marketing your work. The title alone can sell an article—or a book—and keep on selling it. Chapter 9 shows you how to develop your title-writing talents.

Surefire Step #10:
Selling Your Articles

Editors tell stories of having received manuscripts mailed in grocery store sacks tied with string, the text handwritten on yellow legal paper. These manuscripts are not given a second glance, let alone consideration. A professionally submitted manuscript will help you get your manuscript read. Chapter 10 explains the proper manuscript format and how to write cover letters and query letters.

Surefire Step #11:
Exploring the Magazine Marketplace

Each year approximately 45,000 books are published in the United States. Of that number, over 40,000 are nonfiction works. The magazine article business is even better: 90 percent of what magazine editors buy is nonfiction. Ninety percent! And there are over 5,000 magazines to sell to. The problem is finding the *right* magazine for your work. Chapter 11 shows you how to locate the hundreds of lesser-known magazines that are actively seeking and willing to work with new writers.

Surefire Step #12:
Selling Book Ideas

The way to sell a book to publishers is to show them that you have an idea excitingly different from what is already in print, then present that idea in the form of a well-thought-out book proposal. Chapter 12 shows you how to master this critical stage on the road to publication.

These twelve steps to creative and selling success can work for everyone. What writers need most is a book that is written to be understood. Books on writing are too often written on an esoteric level intended to be understood only by the chosen few. Written over the heads of most beginning writers, they are not practical guides to getting published. And that's where this book comes in. It is practical. It is detailed and hands-on. And it is down-to-earth.

I have taught this technique to thousands of students in non-fiction writing classes at the University of California, Santa Barbara, the Adult Education Division of Santa Barbara City College and the Santa Barbara Writers Conference over a ten-year period. Student writers in these classes have written and published dozens of books. Their bylines have appeared in such national magazines as *Ladies' Home Journal, Reader's Digest, The Saturday Evening Post, Vogue, Seventeen, Smithsonian, TV Guide, Modern Maturity, Working Woman* and many others.

The method can't miss. And, using it, neither can you.

1
Unleashing

YOUR CREATIVITY

Successful
Writing Habits

I never quite know when I'm not writing. Sometimes my wife comes up to me at a party and says, "Thurber, stop writing!" She usually catches me in the middle of a paragraph.

—James Thurber

Talent?

Clifton Fadiman, writer, critic, essayist, editor, a man who had conversed with such great writers of this century as William Faulkner, Thomas Mann, and Ernest Hemingway, shrugged at the question. "Talent can be trained or developed," he said. "Perhaps talent is another word for ability or competence." Fadiman paused, then added, "Talent is a very uninteresting word."

Talent . . . an uninteresting word?

No, it is worse. *Talent* is a sneaky, dishonest word. A frightening word that tortures beginning writers who live in dread that they don't have this un-understandable gift from the gods.

Students in my writing classes often ask apprehensively, "Do you think I have talent?" I answer: "If you didn't think you were talented enough to write, you wouldn't be in this class. You'd have signed up for interior design, basket weaving, or oriental rug collecting."

Don't be intimidated by the work of great authors. Nor should you try to emulate the work of today's bestselling writers. No, you may not be able to write nonfiction like Tom Wolfe, Russell Baker, Richard Rhodes, or Joseph Wambaugh, but that doesn't mean you can't write something that will sell.

You don't have to be a fine literary writer to be a selling writer. Most professional writers are not. They are lucid; they write without words getting in their way. Literary writers labor for immortality; selling writers don't have the time.

It's *not* talent that makes a successful writer. It's work. The gods don't give gifts to people who say they want to write, then *never set a word on paper*. And it is not the gods, but editors, who give prizes in the form of bylines for a writer's hard work.

No, success in writing is not a gift from the gods. Writing success derives from the *discipline* needed to set words on paper, the *perseverance* to see a writing project through to its final sale, and most of all, the unwavering *desire* to be a writer. If you have these three qualities, then you can be sure of one thing: People *will* call you gifted or talented.

Discipline

The first American Nobel Prize winner in literature, Sinclair Lewis, was once asked to speak at Columbia University. Striding to the lectern, Lewis glared at his audience, than asked, "How many of you want to be writers? Raise your hands!" A large block of students thrust their hands up. Lewis growled, *"Then why the hell aren't you home writing?"* With that, the great author walked off the stage.

Lewis may have been rude—but he was right. You must discipline yourself to write a specific number of hours each day. That means sitting alone in a room day after day facing a typewriter, or computer screen, or pad of paper, pouring out words.

It's not easy, sitting in solitude in that room, writing. Even bestselling writers like Jackie Collins (*Hollywood Husbands*) have a difficult time coping with the daily task of getting words on paper. Collins says:

> When you're a writer and you wake up, the main thing you want to do is defrost the refrigerator. It seems so much more exciting than shutting yourself up in a study for seven hours. Even if you have a lousy headache or the cat just died, you have to get up and write. I find it incredibly difficult to shut myself away from the world and write.

Few writers confront the typewriter fearlessly. One writer told me, "Writing is like having homework to do for the rest of your life."

Yet the creative process can also be a joy, and completing a well-written manuscript, a delight. And seeing your byline in print for the first time, a moment of sheer ecstasy. (Getting a check for your hard work isn't a bad reward either.)

HOW MUCH TIME EACH DAY MUST YOU WRITE?

Jane Fonda or Richard Simmons can't help anyone build a better body unless that person is willing to spend a specific amount of time *each day* sweating. The same daily regimen must be followed by fledgling writers. Writers should write a minimum of one hour a day, five days a week. *One hour a day, five days a week*. That's not a lot of time to devote to writing. It's like sticking your toe in the water to see if you want to jump in. If the water's fine, you may want to spend more time in the pool.

Professional writers spend anywhere from 8 to 80 hours a week writing. Super-prolific (over 300 books) Isaac Asimov says,

> I can write up to 18 hours a day. Typing 90 words a minute,
> I've done better than 50 pages a day. Nothing interferes

with my concentration. You could put an orgy in my office and I wouldn't look up—well, maybe once.

It's not how many hours you write that counts; it's working *regular hours*—as if you were punching a time clock.

WHEN SHOULD YOU WRITE?

Many successful writers find that the muse joins them in the morning; others write better in the afternoon; still others like to work in the evening. Whatever part of the day you choose to write, make a commitment to be at your writing desk at those times. Then write.

Find a quiet time. If you have children, write after the kids are off to school or when they've gone to bed. Do you have a full-time job? Try writing early in the morning or late in the evening. I know editors who begin their regular office workday at 9:00 a.m.; but they're up long before that, at 5:00 a.m., clicking away at their keyboards, working on their own books. Retired? Start writing today! Now! If you keep saying to yourself that you can't find time to write, you'll never write.

WHERE SHOULD YOU WRITE?

Have a private place to work, a place where you won't be disturbed. A quiet bedroom, the attic, the basement, the kitchen table. Put a sign on the door that says, WARNING: DANGEROUS, WORD-HUNGRY ANIMAL AT WORK! Then take that sign seriously and write!

Writers have differing work habits, but most writers prefer to work in complete seclusion. Author Edna Ferber once said, "The ideal view for daily writing, hour upon hour, is the blank brick wall of a cold-storage warehouse. Failing this, a stretch of sky will do, cloudless if possible."

Harold Robbins, author of such novels as *The Carpetbaggers*, felt the need to be secluded from the world when he wrote. His beautiful villa on the south coast of France had a special room which could be reached only by a retractable ladder. The room's picture window with a view overlooking the Mediterranean distracted him so much that he had it boarded over.

Other writers find that a tranquil view out a window mellows the mind and induces the writing brain cells to produce. Most writers will say, "When I'm looking out the window, I'm working."

WHAT SHOULD YOU WRITE?

Anything. Everything. If you don't have a clear idea of what you want to write, then start by keeping a journal. Write down whatever pops into your mind—what you did the previous day, your feelings about the world situation, what you are going to do tomorrow, your goals. If nothing else, keep up a stream of correspondence to friends and relatives. Your writing will improve. It will become easier, ideas tumbling out on top of one another, the words fighting to get out.

WHAT SHOULD YOU WRITE WITH?

Pen? Pencil? Typewriter? Word processor? Shakespeare didn't do badly with a feathered quill. William Faulkner wrote with a fine pen in tiny script. Hemingway stood at a high desk and meticulously wrote in pencil on a yellow legal pad. John Steinbeck, who also used a pencil, said, "Pencils must be round. A hexagonal one cuts my fingers after a long day."

Typewriters have been around since an English engineer named Henry Hill was granted a patent in 1714 for a machine capable of impressing letters on paper "so neat and exact as not to be distinguished from print." It took the "Type-Writer," as it was named, more than 150 years to find favor with writers. The first author to submit a typed manuscript to a publisher was Mark Twain. (The manuscript may have been *Tom Sawyer*, published in 1876.)

Jackie Collins's method is to write in longhand:

That's the best way to do it; you can write while sitting on an airplane. I used to write my books when I took my kids to school, in the car at stoplights. I write every day of the

week and my secretary comes in once a week and puts
everything on a word processor. I love word processors. I
can't use them but I think they're great. I revise the pages
immediately and my secretary makes the changes without
retyping every page.

Many famous authors, such as Sidney Sheldon and romance writer
Barbara Cartland, dictate manuscripts to their secretaries. No wonder Cartland has over 500 books to her credit! Humorist James
Thurber had his own way of getting words on paper. "My usual
method," he said, "is to spend the mornings turning over the text
in my mind. Then in the afternoon, between two and five, I call
in a secretary and dictate to her. I can do about 2,000 words. It
took me about ten years to learn."

I started my writing career at my dining room table scribbling
with a ballpoint pen on yellow legal paper. I bought a package of
a dozen transparent Bic pens and enjoyed watching the blue ink
in the pens slowly go down as I wrote. (I also had a shoebox in
which I stored the first manuscripts I wrote.) Unfortunately, editors
don't accept handwritten manuscripts, so I learned to punch out
words on an electric typewriter. I eventually switched to a word
processor, which can be a great labor-saving tool for writers.

I wonder what Shakespeare might have accomplished had he
had a computer.

Perseverance

I had an excellent writer in one of my classes who wrote readable,
saleable articles. I suggested that the writer submit one of the
articles to a magazine. The article was rejected. Shocked, the writer
never wrote another creative word. Perseverance means that you
continue writing and submitting your articles no matter how often
those little form rejections show up in the mail. Remember, you
will not be the first writer—or the last—to suffer when an editor

rejects a perfectly good manuscript—that is eventually *sold* to another magazine.

William Saroyan, who wrote the 1940 Pulitzer Prize–winning play, *The Time of Your Life,* got his first acceptance after he'd collected a pile of rejection slips thirty inches high—perhaps 7,000 of them. Jack London's stories were rejected 600 times. (A one-page entry in London's journal tallied fourteen rejections over the two-year period during which the author tried to sell a particular short story. He persistently resubmitted the piece until it sold to *Holiday* magazine for $27.50.)

Remember, don't take rejection personally. When an editor says, "Sorry, it doesn't suit our present needs," keep sending it out until *another* editor says, "I love it. Check's in the mail."

Perseverance also means establishing a goal—and going for it! When I first began my writing career, I was living in Spain and traveling through Europe, so I decided to write travel articles. I bought a copy of *Writer's Market* and spent two days reading all the magazine listings. When I had selected 25 magazines that accepted travel pieces, I set my goal at selling an article to each of those magazines, a goal I came close to accomplishing within the next five years. Many times I made more than one sale to the same magazine, and in a few cases established a lasting—and profitable—relationship with the editor.

Tape this goal-setting note on your typewriter:

IF YOU DON'T KNOW WHERE YOU'RE GOING,
THEN YOU'RE ALREADY THERE!

Then make a list of writing goals to be accomplished on a daily, weekly, monthly and annual basis. Each time you accomplish one of your goals, mark through it with a pen.

Desire

I like the quote from writer Fannie Hurst: "I'm not happy when I'm writing, but I'm more unhappy when I'm not." You don't have to be an unhappy writer to be a successful one, but you do have to have a strong desire to become a writer—a deep, gut feeling that says you want this more than anything else in your life. Ray Bradbury says you have to "cry" for it.

Okay, so you've got the desire to write, and you can discipline yourself to sit at your writing space for at least one hour a day, and you are a persevering, goal-setting person.

Now it's time to start putting black on white.

The Creative Impulse

I listen to the voices.

—William Faulkner

N ow you're ready. You're sitting at your writing desk, ready to begin writing the next *New York Times* bestseller—but there is one tiny little problem . . . You've got writer's block.

Or so you say.

There's a Writer on the Block

In ancient Egypt writer's block was a twenty-ton hunk of sandstone with hieroglyphics chipped into its surface. Today, writer's block is an excuse for not writing. Writers have used this ploy—an esoteric, vaguely psychological-sounding affliction—to convince nonwriters to feel sorry for them. Other writers have perpetuated the myth, knowing they may need it themselves someday.

Writer's block seldom occurs in writers working under a deadline. Reporters, technical writers, business writers and advertising copywriters all know writer's block by another name: unemployment.

Think of writer's block as a myth, an excuse some writers use to justify not producing. When their fingers show up for work, their minds are out to lunch. Instead of writing, they busy themselves by scribbling *"Gone With the Wind"* on a scrap of paper and putting their byline beneath it. Perhaps they put off writing by conducting a pencil-sharpening ritual with the dozen pencils stacked in a vase, or making a second cup of strong coffee, even though they can't stand coffee.

Sure, it can be tough getting started. Even famous writers of the past tried all sorts of gimmicks to avoid what they thought of as writer's block. Jack London had one glass of wine before he took pen in hand. The Russian writer Gogol kept a desk drawer full of rotting apples because their odor inspired him.

Some writers take a brisk walk before confronting the typewriter; others play deafening music while writing; and some have been known to set an alarm that spurs them to begin. Then there was the writer who devised the most explosive way to begin a writing project: he fired a pistol into the air.

Getting Those First Words on Paper

Do not fall into the trap of blaming lack of production on outside influences. Certainly there are times when we are stuck for words and that's frustrating. But there are ways to kick-start yourself. Here are a few:

1. Sit at the typewriter whether you write or not.
2. Develop a self-start booster shot to get the first words on paper. Somerset Maugham would take up his fountain pen and write at the top of the page: "My name is Somerset Maugham, I live in a villa in the south of France, and I collect paintings . . ." By the third line Maugham was working on the project he had in mind.

3. To gain access to the ideas and images waiting to spring from your mind, write nonstop for ten minutes. Write about the chair you're sitting on. Don't stop, not even if the telephone rings. Don't correct typos. If you get stuck, write about getting stuck.

4. Write about *not* being able to write. This is what I have student writers do when they can't get started. I've had papers turned in to class that began:

My writing instructor told me to write, to put words on paper, any words. Well, here they are, just words, nonsense words about not being able to write. This doesn't sound like it's going to work, but I will keep writing until this begins to make sense . . . Sense . . . now that's what my neighbor never had much of, he was a blind carpenter who worked with buzz saws . . .

And the writer was off—and writing.

5. Talk your writing project into a tape recorder. Many times we can articulate what we want to say more easily than we can write it. Using a tape recorder can help bring into focus what you want to get across. In talking about your idea, you may find a simpler, clearer way of saying it. You may even learn to dictate your work, as Sidney Sheldon does.

A warning: Don't talk too much to others about your story before writing it down. Telling somebody the story can weaken one's resolve to put it on paper.

6. Don't complete a day's work. Leave the story hanging, even in midsentence, and pick up where you left off the next day.

7. Reread the previous day's work. It's a good way to refresh your mind about the story you are working on.

8. Have several writing projects going at once. If one project stalls, work on another.

9. Create an idea file. Reading through the file can inspire you to write.

10. Use a reward system. For completing the first draft of a magazine article, open a chilled bottle of wine, go to a movie you've wanted to see, buy a book you've wanted to read.

11. Read everything: magazines, newspapers, old yearbooks. You can learn and be stimulated by reading books and magazines about writing.

12. Take correspondence courses, attend seminars, workshops, writers' conferences. Enroll in a writing class at college or through an adult education program. A creative writing class will help you develop discipline and provide incentive to help you write. Writers keep coming back to my writing classes, not to hear the same lecture (or old jokes), but as a form of discipline.

Writing is a lonely trade. But you can unleash your creativity with these simple tools.

Writers talk about the power of the elusive muse, or speak in awe about inspiration striking like a glittering bolt from the sky. Unfortunately, that lightning strikes far too seldom. How can we grab the creative impulse by the throat and make it work for us? You can help unleash your own creativity when you learn to use two more writing concepts: inspiration and imagery.

Inspiration

Author Barnaby Conrad was a 30-year-old unknown writer in 1952 when he wrote his bestselling novel, *Matador*. While writing the novel, the creative impulse was so strong it took Conrad only eight weeks to finish the manuscript. Here's how he described the way inspiration drove him during the creation of *Matador:*

For some reason the writing process was different than it had ever been. I seemed to have caught fire, a feverish compulsion that I'd never really felt before. When I sat at the typewriter I didn't ask myself "How would Hemingway phrase this or Fitzgerald or Sinclair Lewis?" but only what was the true or graphic way to say what I wanted to say. Day after day the exhilarating process went on.

How do we tap our own inspiration and make it work for us? For most writers it's through hard work. Some writers find their inspiration in gardening or standing on a hill watching clouds. Tennessee Williams said, "All you have to do is close your eyes and wait for the symbols." That may have been fine for Williams, but what about us? Is there a method we can use to release elusive inspiration? Yes, but in doing so, we must first delve into the right brain.

WRITING WITH THE RIGHT SIDE OF THE BRAIN

Have you ever driven on an interstate highway, become lost in thought, and suddenly discovered that you had arrived at your destination? How did you get there? You don't remember passing cars, seeing road signs . . . How? The two hemispheres of your brain, working in conjunction, got you there. The left brain, the analytical hemisphere, took over the driving responsibilities and allowed the right brain to enter the realm of fantasy. (Note: I *do not* recommend this as a method for conceiving writing ideas. Dreaming and driving don't mix!)

What exactly does the left brain do? The left brain specializes in such capabilities as:

- Verbal skills
- Analytical concepts
- Linear arrangement (a one-step-at-a-time way of thinking)
- Mathematical problems

The right brain is concerned with:

- Images
- Imaginative concepts
- Spatial relationships (such as working jigsaw puzzles)
- Metaphoric values (to understand the difference between what is said and what is meant)
- Emotional processes
- Dreams

How can we, as writers, unleash the creative impulses of the right brain?

Many writers who have exercised the right brain for years say they can turn it on at will, like clicking a switch on the side of their head. Before writing, they visualize the scene, characters or events they are going to describe, then settle into a semidream state. Their mind becomes a motion picture camera, flickering scenes into the subconscious. The fingers take over and transfer those visual thoughts to a keyboard, onto paper and eventually into the reader's mind.

When a writer is deep within this creative mode, he is rarely disturbed by outside distractions. I know my wife can call me from the kitchen and I won't hear her. A baby can cry and it won't disturb me. (However, if the telephone rings, I am shaken back to reality. After all, it could be an editor or a publisher calling.)

There are several practical ways to learn to shift into the right brain and stimulate creativity: stream-of-consciousness writing; boring the left brain; and taking an imagery trip.

STREAM-OF-CONSCIOUSNESS WRITING

Stream-of-consciousness composition is an unstructured writing activity that will force you to swing from an analytical mode into a creative, right-brain mode of thought.

The sinews of a writer's mind, like an athlete's muscles, need some stretching before they begin to function smoothly. Some writers use the stream-of-consciousness method to unlock their inspiration. The writer, keeping in mind the scene he is working on, begins writing anything that comes into his mind—words, phrases, sentences, nonsense. He does not pause to correct grammar or spelling. Occupied with the single goal of writing, the conscious mind relaxes and allows the mind to enter the realm of the right brain. After five to ten minutes of these mental gymnastics, the writer is ready to take off on a productive creative journey.

BORING THE LEFT BRAIN

How can we bore the left brain until it becomes tired and gives up? If we stare at a drawing of a spoked wheel, for example, the left brain analyzes the wheel: the number of spokes, its circumference, its diameter, until there is nothing more to analyze. Bored, it shuts down. Then the right brain clicks in. The wheel is now a space ship hurtling toward a new planet in another galaxy, a Frisbee tossed into the sky . . .

What happens when we are reading a book and suddenly realize we're at the bottom of the page and can't remember the previous paragraphs? What happened to our mind? What were we thinking? Certainly not about what the writer was trying to tell us. The left brain had become so bored with the writing (not a good sign for the author of the book) that we slipped into fantasyland—and activated the right brain.

TAKING AN IMAGERY TRIP

Meditation and yoga are methods of boring the left brain and entering a different kind of awareness. The images created during these moments of deep reflection linger with us like vibrant pages from an illustrated book. Can we apply this to writing? Sure. Let's take a quick imagery trip and see how it works:

We close our eyes and imagine ourselves walking through a forest; hearing, seeing, touching. We can see the sun's rays slanting through the canopy of leaves, feel the rough bark of the trees as we pass, hear a bubbling stream before us. We step on the flat stones in the narrow waterway and cross to the other side. Climbing up a grassy embankment, we see a wide meadow, the lush grass undulating in the breeze. In the distance is a house. We walk toward it through the tall grass. The chimney emits a curl of white smoke, the door is ajar. We push open the door. Inside we see . . .

What did you see inside the house?

Perhaps a rocking chair, a braided rug, a fire in the fireplace, a woman stirring a pot, a little girl cuddling a doll . . . Whatever you saw, you created by using your right brain.

As with any other skill, using the right brain takes practice. Learn this valuable technique by visualizing different scenes and it will soon become automatic. Next time you are daydreaming, remember that it's your right brain at work.

Imagery

In a "Family Circus" cartoon one of the children is holding a book and looking at his mother. The child says, "I like to read. It makes me see pictures."

Pictures: that's what a writer is trying to create in the reader's mind. Pictures. How does a writer learn to open this window of creativity for the reader? By using imagery in his writing.

Here's a scene from *Nightwing* by Martin Cruz Smith:

The Red Man tobacco sign—an Indian profile with a corroded eye—stared west. Two pickup trucks rusted in a bower of yellow creosote bushes. Out of a headlight socket flicked the quick ribbon of a lizard's tongue.

It was noon in the painted desert. A hundred degrees.

The tobacco sign and car hoods welded together in upright rows were the walls of Abner Tasupi's shed. A square of sheet steel was the roof. Sometimes, Abner fixed cars, and sometimes, he sold Enco gasoline straight from a drum. Usually, the drums were empty and he spent the day listening to his transistor radio. They had Navajo disc jockeys on a Gallup station. While he hated Navajos, there were no Hopi disc jockeys. There were lots of Hopis back up in Black Mesa, but not one that dared come visit him.

Well, one.

Youngman Duran sat in the shed between the erupting springs of a car seat. A half-empty jug of Gallo port nestled between his legs.

"I'm sorry," Abner apologized to his only friend, "but they got to die."

"Anyone I know?"

Note how Martin Cruz Smith uses vivid words that evoke images and sensations. We can *see* the rusting pickups, the tobacco sign, the lizard in the broken headlight, Abner's shed, and we can *feel* the heat. Cruz Smith has *shown* us this scene from the painted desert.

The old writing cliché "show, don't tell" is a cliché because it's true. The concept is as valid today as it was when the Egyptians first inscribed hieroglyphics in their tombs. What is the difference between *show* and *tell?* This is *telling:*

The teacher walked *angrily* down the hall.

This is *showing:*

The teacher bulldozed her way through a circle of startled students as she stalked toward the principal's office.

Similarly, this is *showing:*

The teacher banged several locker doors shut, jarring nearby students as she strode toward the principal's office.

The reader can "see" the teacher's anger.

Want to *show* the opulence of a sheik's desert palace? Have pink flamingos strutting down the marble hallways.

Or dip your finger into the palace's shimmering pool of liquid mercury. And then *show* what it *feels* like.

THE FIVE SENSES

We entered a darkness of brick and soot-blackened windows, a cavern of hammers and forges, a huge smithy. Steam locomotives long and looming as ocean liners could be clocked around on track sections within its vastness and repaired. The forges glowed like campfires. The hammer faces rang like bells and threw firefalls of iron sparks. Sulfur and iron gritted the air, cinders of coal smoke scratched my eyes . . .

This Dickensian vision was written in 1990 by Richard Rhodes in his book, *A Hole in the World: An American Boyhood*. Note how Rhodes helps the reader visualize the scene by using the five senses: sight, sound, smell, touch, taste. You can see the hugeness of the locomotives, hear the hammers, smell and taste the sulfur in the air and touch the coal cinders. With the use of the senses any writer can convey the feeling of a scene and make it become visually alive.

Here is an example that shows a single scene rewritten three times. Note that the first draft simply *tells* the reader what is happening. The second draft improves on that and begins to show the scene. The final draft uses the different senses, plus dialogue, to show the scene more vividly.

1. *First Draft:*

The carnival grounds were crowded with people that hot, humid afternoon.

2. Second Draft:

The fat man pushed his way through the crowd to the refreshment stand to buy a snow cone. Several sweating people grumbled at the intrusion.

3. Third Draft:

"Get your ice-cold snow cones!"
    The clash of music—pipe organs on the left, *La Bamba* on the right—almost drowned out the carnival barker's sales pitch. Shoving his way past a kid clutching two quarters, the fat man leaned his elbow on the high counter. Sweat dripped from his chin onto the metal surface as he slapped a dollar down. "Gimmie one of them cherry flavors!" The crowd folded in around him, then gave way. The scent of the sugar and syrup failed to mask the odor of his sweat-darkened shirt.

Let images form in your mind as you are writing. Close your eyes and use your mind like a movie camera. See the scene, then let the images travel through your fingers to the pen and onto the paper. Here are three exercises in imagery that will help you create vivid and fully realized scenes.

IMAGERY EXERCISE #1

Sit at your writing desk or on the couch. Grab pen and paper. Relax, open up your mind and write these two words on a piece of paper:

LITTLE GIRL

What image do these words create in your mind? Perhaps they recall a little girl you once knew, perhaps a fantasy child—perhaps yourself. What else could the two words mean?
    Now write these words on the paper:

DUSTY ATTIC

Do you have a visual impression of a dusty attic, or do the

words conjure other images? Little girl, dusty attic . . . What do you see?

Ready for the last two words? When you have all six on paper, begin writing—immediately. Incorporate the three phrases in what you write. Write anything you want, whatever comes to mind. Here we go:

WHITE BONES

I use this exercise in my nonfiction writing classes. To relax the writer, I ask that the pieces be turned in anonymously. Many times the results of this exercise show unique creativity. Some students respond simply:

> The *little girl* climbed up to the *dusty attic* and saw some *white bones*.

More often than not the completed exercise will read something like this:

> The *little girl* had been told by her mother never to go into the *dusty attic*. One day, overcome by her curiosity, the girl sneaked up the stairs and peeked into the dusty space. In one corner she saw an old trunk. When she opened the lid, she saw the *white bones* of a long-dead rat.

There's nothing wrong with that—the writer devised a visual scene. Many times, however, the six words unleash creative impulses that are original—and surprising:

> The *little girl* trembled while waiting for the massive front door to open. After all, it was her first Halloween night out alone and her skeleton costume seemed quite silly. Worse yet, she had outgrown it.
>
> The door suddenly opened and the hall light silhouetted

a huge man who said in a gruff voice, "Those *white bones* don't scare me, little girl. What's your name?"

"Dusty," she said, *"Dusty Attic."*

A wonderful and completely visual scene. Here's another very different response:

Amy was a very special *little girl* who lived in an ordinary house on an ordinary street. What made Amy so special was her two cats. Her black cat was called *Dusty Attic*, for he had the most extraordinary eyes that were pale blue and seemed to cloud over as though they held some mysterious secret. Her white cat was named *White Bones* because no matter how much cat food the animal ate she always stayed skinny, her ribs showing through her fur.

Got the picture? Like to try another?

THREE PEOPLE

BLACK CAR

RETURN HOME

(One of the shortest and most clever responses I got back read: "If *three people* leave in a *black car*, and one of them is Jimmy Hoffa, only two people will *return home*.")

Try this one:

TRAIN STATION

SMALL BOY

GOLDEN CHAIN

IMAGERY EXERCISE #2

To loosen up your right brain, write 250 words (about one double-spaced manuscript page) describing one of three kinds of scene:

1. The scene can be real. Sit in a park and describe what you see. Go to a bus station, walk on the beach, look out your living room window. (One student sat in front of her

closet and described the contents in detail, another showed in agonizing detail how she picked a large scab off her knee. It was *very* visual.)

2. Fantasize. Make up a scene in your mind.

3. Visualize a scene from the past. Picture something that happened to you, an event from the past that made a deep impression on you.

Here's an example of a scene recalled from the past:

Walking down the dusty main street, the damp gunnysack tossed over one shoulder, the boy saw old Crazy Joe sitting in front of the drugstore.

"Hullo there, young'un," Old Crazy said. "What'cha got in that sack?"

"Crawdads. Got 'em down by the creek. Goin' fishin' with 'em soon's I get my pole."

Old Crazy sucked on his front teeth. "Wouldn't happen to have an extra, some old granddaddy crawdaddy?" He chuckled and puffed out his cheeks like Popeye.

The boy knew what was coming and opened the sack. There was the smell of damp moss and he could see the squirming crawfish in the dim light crawling endlessly over one another. Reaching into the sack, he eyed his quarry and pinched its hard tail between his fingers. Claws flailing, the crawdad came out into the sunlight. Crazy Joe's eyes widened.

"Well, yes sir, boy, that's one fine-looking crawdad."

The boy handed it to him and waited expectantly. Old Crazy ripped the claws off the slimy creature—then stuffed it into his mouth. He cracked the shell between his few remaining teeth and sucked on the tender exposed tail meat. The boy watched, the juice in his own mouth beginning to form. Finally, Old Crazy spit what was left of the shell out of his mouth.

"Wouldn't happen to have another, would ya, boy?"

See how it's done? This writer's right brain kicked into high gear and the images poured out, picking up speed as the words came. Sit at your typewriter, relax, close your eyes and visualize a scene from your childhood, then begin typing. Or fantasize. Ease into the right brain and make up a scene filled with people and places. Or grab a pen and paper, walk downtown or into a grassy park, and like an artist sketching a scene on an art board with charcoal, create a picture—with words. Do ten or twenty of these imagery exercises and you'll see your writing improve.

By using these elements of inspiration and imagery you can unleash your creativity and give your writing wings. Like Daedalus, fashion your own wings—and fly.

Basic Writing Techniques

Type on one side of the page, double-spaced, and leave wide margins.

—Raymond Chandler

B efore you begin writing one word, you must realize that you have your own built-in style. You were born with it. You can alter that style to make what you write more readable, but you can't change it completely. You could never have William Faulkner's style. Nor William Styron's, Joan Didion's or Tom Wolfe's. You might "parrot" one of these writers, but never write in their style.

Discovering Your Style

At the opposite ends of the writing spectrum are two styles: academic and breezy.

ACADEMIC STYLE

To illustrate the staid, academic (perhaps "stuffy" is a better word) style, here's a clip that appeared in a newspaper:

Whether one is dealing with the treatment of the common cold or of cancer, and whether one is dealing with a benign vitamin or a highly toxic chemotherapy program, it would seem to serve the interest of the patient best for public advocacy of a proposed treatment to be withheld until that treatment has been proven effective by definitive studies of sound scientific design.

Yawn . . .

BREEZY STYLE

At the other end of the spectrum is the bright and breezy style of writing, the "Gosh, how ya doin', ole buddy?" style best suited to a fraternity newsletter. Here's an example:

If you want to be a rich, pretentious snot—and who doesn't?—you should learn about wine. Alternatively, you can buy polo ponies, but the wine approach is better because you won't have to spend weekends shoveling huge quantities of polo pony waste out of the rec room. . . .

Obviously, if you are going to sell your writing to major magazines, you want to avoid a style that is either too breezy or too academic. You have to develop a style that is entertaining and readable, not boring or embarrassing.

Here is a chart of writing styles showing the range of editorial preference for a few publications. If you want to write lively, readable material written for a wide general audience, your writing style should fall somewhere in the middle. Read magazines of this type to see where your style fits.

BREEZY ← ——————————————————————————————→ ACADEMIC

fraternity newsletters   *The Atlantic*
          Cosmopolitan   university textbooks
              McCall's   technical publications
     joke books   *Playboy*
        greeting cards   *Saturday Review*
                    Reader's Digest   literary magazines
     confession magazines   *Vanity Fair*
        National Enquirer   *Parade*
               The Saturday Evening Post
                         Harper's Magazine
              Family Circle
        detective magazines   company brochures
                    Travel & Leisure
                    TWA Ambassador

Your style of writing may lean toward the academic (and the more literary) or toward the breezy and more colloquial. *Cosmopolitan*'s general writing style is certainly more lively than *McCall's*, for instance, and the *Reader's Digest*'s is breezier than the *Saturday Review*'s.

THE FOG FACTOR IN WRITING STYLE

Somerset Maugham said that the important elements in writing are "clarity, simplicity, euphony and liveliness." Unfortunately, in the process of trying to construct each phrase or sentence like a work of art, too many writers forget that effective writing must be readable. To be obscure, to let your writing become fogbound, is not a virtue.

Here's an excerpt from Daniel Defoe's classic, *Robinson Crusoe*. The scene takes place after Crusoe had been tossed from his ship during a violent storm. There's something unusual about this paragraph. See if you can discover what.

> I did my best to float on the top, and held my breath to do so. The next wave was quite as high, and shut me up in its bulk. I held my hands down to my side, and then my head shot out of the top of the waves. This gave me heart and breath too, and soon my feet felt the ground.

Got it? *All the words are in one syllable.* No, that's not the way Defoe wrote it. The book was rewritten by a writer named Mary Godolphin and published in 1882 under the title, *Robinson Crusoe in Words of One Syllable.*

Abraham Lincoln's Second Inaugural Address was a marvel of simplicity. Of the 701 words, 550 were words of one syllable.

Simplicity: that's the name of the selling writer's game. You don't have to dog-ear your dictionary searching for mile-long words with multisyllabic sounds—words like pneumonoultramicroscopicsilicovolcanoconiosis (the longest word in *Webster's Third New International Dictionary,* which it defines as a miner's lung disease).

Keep it simple. And readable.

Beginnings

RESEARCH

An editor for whom I had written several magazine articles called me and in a breathless voice said, "Help! I need a feature piece for my Easter issue. Can you do an article on Easter eggs?"

"Decorating Easter eggs?" I asked, thinking that my children liked to make funny faces on Easter eggs by cutting colored pieces of felt and pasting on hair, hats, cheeks and mouths.

"Perfect!" the editor said.

"But it's December," I protested. I realized magazines needed seasonal pieces months in advance, but colored eggs at Christmas . . . ?

"Right . . . need the article in two weeks." Click.

Decorating eggs wasn't a problem, as my children joyously combined the idea of Santa Claus with a yuletide Easter Bunny—but what did I know about eggs? I went to the library, and after thumbing through several books on the subject, found that "eggery," the art of decorating an egg, had been practiced since the time of the Romans and had continued throughout the centuries until the Russians developed it into a fine art in the nineteenth century. With this research material I was able to write an article titled "Easter Eggheads."

Writers are gatherers of information. We need to have many facts at hand to complete a particular writing project. Some of that information comes from our own personal experience and knowledge, and some can be attained by using research sources.

What's the best method for researching an idea? First, learn to love your librarian. Librarians are professional people who are gratified when anyone (especially a writer) asks them for help. They view their work as a *service*. Walk up to your librarian at the reference desk and say, "I'm a writer and I need information for a magazine article I'm working on . . ." You'll make their day. Your own, too.

If you know nothing about library research, *Finding Facts Fast* by Alden Todd (Ten Speed Press) offers excellent insights on library research methods and techniques.

You can do some of the work yourself. The *Reader's Guide to Periodical Literature* is a great library source for looking up a specific subject that has been written about in major magazines and journals. This listing, which is updated monthly, indexes material by subject and author. When you find an article you need, see if your library carries back issues, or if it's available from the publisher or other source. If your library does have it, make notes on 3x5 cards or use the photocopy machine to record the information you need.

Ask your reference librarian for access to R. R. Bowker's *Books in Print*. It lists all books currently available by subject, title and author. Check the library's card file to see which of the books on your subject are available.

Try the *Magazine Index* to find articles published in popular magazines.

The *UPI News Index* will get you subject listings that are as recent as today's newspaper.

Newsearch and *National Newspaper Index* will tell you about subjects that are listed in major newspapers like the *New York Times* and the *Los Angeles Times*.

After exhausting your library, write for *Selected U.S. Government Publications* (Superintendent of Documents, U.S.G.P.O., P.O. Box 1821, Washington, D.C. 20402) for a monthly catalogue of pamphlets on a wide variety of subjects. *The United States Government Manual*, which is published annually, provides information on all three government branches and lists a wealth of agencies and phone numbers.

What do you do when the information you need cannot be found in magazines or books? Interview an expert. Many professional people, teachers, attorneys, physicians and businesspeople are willing to make themselves available to an enterprising writer with a tape recorder. *You* may not be an authority on your subject, but your high school or college friend, your neighbor or coworker may be. Any one of these acquaintances may have the special knowledge you need to conduct an interview so you can add extra credibility to your article. Be sure to approach any and all potential interviewees with tact and courtesy; you'll be surprised at how willing to be interviewed most will be.

Here's a source of research that few writers consider: television. Instead of using your video to tape *As the World Turns*, record a personality or expert being interviewed on a talk show. Not only will you get the information you need, you'll be able to observe the expert in action.

Research sources abound, from tourist agencies, to government offices, to historical societies. A little digging will unearth a myriad of facts that can make your article come alive.

WRITING FROM RESEARCH

Once you've gathered all the information you want, you'll need to incorporate it into your writing. The first thing to remember is that you don't have to use every word you've collected. Don't overburden your text with too many boring details. Remember, you want your writing to be entertaining, not to deliver fact after fact like a textbook. (The facts should be the raisins, not the pudding.)

When quoting from the experts, select a line that best illustrates the central idea of your article. When quoting from other sources (magazines or books), list the title and author of the piece. Do not footnote (unless you are writing a textbook or know that the magazine you are writing for requires it).

The easiest way to assure that you present all your information *in an organized manner* is to outline the article.

OUTLINING AN ARTICLE

Most writers try to wing it. "Nah . . . I don't need an outline," they say. "That's for professors and college students. I just sit down at my typewriter and out come the words."

It's not enough to throw together a random set of statements and call it an article. You need to arrange your ideas according to a writing "map." Outlining will help you find a pattern for the pieces of information you intend to include and make the writing flow more smoothly.

A magazine article outline can be relatively simple. It doesn't have to be extensive or have Roman numeral subheadings. Just pick out the eight or ten points you are going to cover in the article and put them on paper. Write down how you want to begin the piece, then the sequence you plan to use for the material you have available. During the writing you may discover that you need to change the sequence.

Start with:

1. The title.
2. The introduction. (What will interest your readers the most?)
3. The body, which will include all your research material. You may want to use quotes from interviews, anecdotes and dialogue in the text. List these items separately in your outline.
4. The conclusion.

You may have information that doesn't fit into your outline, such as historical notes, or a list of restaurants or hotels (if you're writing a travel article). That information can be included in *sidebars*, those color-coded or framed boxes that appear on the printed page of the magazine. To indicate to an editor that that is what you have in mind, add a manuscript page to the end of the article and label it "Sidebar."

Choosing Person and Tense

After you have completed your outline and before you begin writing, there are two important decisions to be made: from whose point of view do you want to write, and what verb tense do you want to use?

First, Second, or Third Person?

WRITING IN THE FIRST PERSON

A personal experience story is generally told in the first person. However, the writer must be careful. The single most frequently used word in the English language is "I." Its overuse can make the writer sound egocentric—and make the reader lose interest.

If you decide to use the first person, go back over the first few pages of the manuscript and circle every "I" on the page. If the page looks like a bowl of Cheerios, then you've used too many "I's."

Here's an example of the beginning of an article on Julia Child which is told in the first person. Note that the word "I" is only used one time.

> "Sorry, we're having a bit of trouble with our oven," Julia Child says in a chortle that could curdle cooling Béarnaise sauce. She shakes my hand, pulls me through the open front door of her home, and propels me into the living room. "Seems rather foolish, a cook without an oven," she adds, then pops into the kitchen just as the oven repairman pops out. I follow her through the swinging door.

Note: before deciding to use the first person, make sure the magazine (or magazines) you plan on submitting to accepts first-person pieces.

WRITING IN THE SECOND PERSON

The second person, "you," is rarely used throughout a complete article. The constant repetition of the word "you" is eventually intrusive. However, when used in an article lead it does have the effect of bringing the reader into the story as the scene unfolds. Here's a lead from a profile on the actor Karl Malden which uses this technique.

> Karl Malden pads toward you in stocking feet. He looks just as you'd expected: tall, with the face of Everyman. He could pass for the owner of the mom and pop grocery store on the corner, your bank teller, a country doctor, a minister . . .

Once the actual question/answer session of the interview with Malden began, the use of the second person was dropped and the third person was used.

WRITING IN THE THIRD PERSON

This is the voice in which most nonfiction articles are written. The writer stands back, acts as an observer and narrates. Here is an example of the use of the third person from an article on Spanish sherry wine:

> A certain ancient sherry, glistening in its tulip-shaped *copa*, is held to the light and admired for its golden color flecked with specks of purple. Its bouquet and flavor is rich and heavy—a tiny sip covers the tip of the tongue and makes one marvel that the sun that warmed it to life in the Andalusian vineyard was the same sun that beamed on the Spanish Armada, Queen Elizabeth, and Sir Walter Raleigh four hundred years ago.

Verb Tense: Present or Past?

USING THE PRESENT TENSE

In the present tense the action appears to be going on at the very moment the reader reads the words. For example:

> Robert Redford *sits* in front of a blazing fireplace.

The reader has the illusion of seeing the scene as it unfolds. The present tense is an effective way of bringing the reader into the picture. (Note that the previous examples on Julia Child and Karl Malden also used the present tense.)

USING THE PAST TENSE

In this approach, the action takes place in the recent past:

> Robert Redford *sat* in front of a blazing fireplace.

Caution: Once you have established the tense, stick with it. Here is an incorrect use of tense:

Robert Redford *sat* in front of the blazing fireplace waiting for the servant to bring his scotch and water. When he *arrives*, Redford *told* the servant he *wants* a glass of brandy instead.

This is not to say you can't change tenses in an article. You may start with an action sequence in the present tense, then use a flashback, written in the past tense, to provide background information that leads up to the action.

Grammar, Syntax, Punctuation

Relatives of 87-year-old Clara Bell Webb said today she continued to operate the tiny downtown grocery store where she was killed Saturday, "more or less to have something to do."

This scrambled syntax shows that certain rules of English usage are necessary to make your writing clear. But don't get bogged down with them. Did you know there are 300 or so rules governing English grammar—rules so complicated that they drive some writing students away?

I know.

Ten years before I changed careers and became a full-time writer, I decided to brush up on my grammar and enrolled in an extension course—Composition 101. The rules I encountered were so stifling, so terrifying, I didn't write creatively for years.

Remember this: writing *is not* grammar, syntax or punctuation. Writing *is* getting one pure idea out of your head, or one pure emotion out of your heart, then putting that idea or emotion on paper so the reader can share it.

Want to learn grammatical style? Then read. Read books by famous authors. Note how they *break* the rules of grammar. And yes, you too can break the rules—as long as you know them in the first place.

When asked how he handled the rules of grammar in the 300 books he has written, author Isaac Asimov replied:

> I don't know any but the simplest rules of English grammar, and I seldom consciously apply them. Nevertheless, I instinctively write correctly and, I like to think, in an interesting fashion. I know when something sounds right and when it doesn't, and I can tell the difference without hesitation, even when writing at breakneck speed. How do I do this? I haven't the faintest idea.

No, I am not advocating that writers disregard the rules of good writing. Good usage means easy reading. There will be many rules that a fledgling writer will need to have at his fingertips. For instance: How should you handle the title of a book in a typed manuscript? (*Answer:* You underline it to show that it will be italicized in print.) How do you indicate the title of a magazine article? (*Answer:* You use quotation marks.)

That's it! That's about all I want to tell you, as this is not a textbook on English grammar. There are many manuals available that you can get for your writer's reference shelf. Some examples are: *A Manual for Writers* by Kate L. Turabian, or *Write Right* by Jan Venolia, a good digest of punctuation, grammar and style. *The Transitive Vampire: A Grammar Handbook for the Innocent, the Eager, and the Doomed* by Karen Elizabeth Gordon has some of the most amusing and peculiar grammatical examples in print.

Aside from a dictionary and a thesaurus, you should also have the book that professional writers consider the mini-bible of writing, *Elements of Style*, by William Strunk, Jr., and E. B. White.

Whatever books you decide to keep handy for quick reference, any compendium of lexicographical lore can be of great help to a writer.

. . .

The basic mechanics of writing will help you achieve the style you need to sell your magazine article. What the editor reads must appear to be a smooth-flowing, sensibly organized, readable piece of writing. Only *you* should know it was hard work. As Somerset Maugham said, "A good style should show no sign of effort. What is written should seem a happy accident."

The Idea Factory

Everything has been thought of before, but the problem is to think of it again.

—Goethe

Y ou're sitting in the waiting room of your dentist's office thumbing through a magazine when your interest is piqued by an article titled, "Backpacking Trails in the Sierra Nevadas." Great! You're a hiking enthusiast. Three months earlier you went on the same backpacking trip. You read the article. Finishing the last sentence you say to yourself, "I could write a better story than that." Then you remind yourself that it's already been done.

Wait! You *can* write that backpacking story. Magazine article *ideas* cannot be copyrighted. If they were protected there would be few, if any, subjects left to write about. You can write on the same subject, but with a different angle or focus. For instance, here are five different slants on the backpacking story:

1. Three Great Backpacking Trails
2. Today's Hottest Backpacking Trails

3. Backpacking Trails for the Adventurous
4. The Beginner's Guide to Backpacking Trails
5. The Experts Talk about Backpacking Trails

That's only the beginning. There are hundreds of slants you can use to write articles about backpacking—everything from "Cooking out of a Backpack" to "Packing a Backpack." That article you read in the dentist's office shouldn't discourage you from writing; rather, it should *impel* you to write your own article.

Look at it this way. *You don't get an idea; you recognize an idea.*

When I began writing, I lived in southern Spain near Jerez de la Frontera, the center of the world's sherry wine production. I became enamored of the sherry-making process, and toured the many *bodegas* (wineries) that produced the golden wine. I didn't consider writing about sherry until I saw an article in a food and wine magazine on the subject. I said to myself, *I know more about sherry than that writer!* That's when I recognized sherry as a subject worth writing about. I began a series of articles, each with a different slant.

The first was an overall look at sherry: "Sherry—The Golden Wine of Spain."

The second was a tour through a sherry *bodega*: "Sherry, the Noble Wine."

The third explored the uniqueness of the wine: "The Secrets of Sherry."

Then came a travel story about the city where sherry is made: "Jerez de la Frontera: The Sherry Citadel of Spain."

The next delved into the family history behind one of the great *bodegas*: "A Sherry Dynasty."

Other slants followed: "The Sherry Harvest Festival," "Sherry Brandy," "American Sherry," "Cooking with Sherry," all of which were sold as magazine articles, then collected into a book, *Sherry: The Golden Wine of Spain*. And it all started with my recognizing an idea in an article I read in a magazine.

Getting Great Ideas

Why do readers read? Editors tell us there are four main reasons:

1. To be entertained
2. To learn
3. To share an experience
4. To be up on what's new

Whatever idea you come up with, check it against the above list. And remember—just because you're writing nonfiction doesn't mean you're not an entertainer. If the reader learns something from your writing, and is *also* entertained, you're going to collect a lot of bylines.

What's the difference between an ordinary idea and a terrific one? A good idea will keep you awake during the day, but a great idea will keep you awake all night. Where do you find these great ideas? Do they pop into your mind like magic? Do you sit at your typewriter waiting for inspiration to strike? Do you edge closer to the telephone, hoping someone will call with an idea? If that's what you think, you have a long wait ahead.

You must set up your own "idea factory."

Here are four steps that will provide the key to unlocking the door to that factory:

1. *Write down five items you know well enough to conduct a class in.* We're talking about easy things here, not how to design a nuclear reactor. Each of us has learned many skills. Ask yourself, "What have I learned in life that I know how to do as well, or better, than others?" What about your schooling? Your hobbies? Perhaps you love to

crochet afghans, weave baskets, collect stamps. Could you teach these skills to someone else?

2. *Write down five magazines you enjoy reading*. These are the first magazines you will want to write for. Your ideas will fit into those magazines because the editors' tastes already reflect your interests. Develop at least one saleable idea for each magazine.

3. *Write down five magazine articles you have found fascinating*. Analyze each story, making a list of the points that grabbed and held your attention. These observations will give you a "fascination" standard against which you can compare your own writing.

4. *Finally, write down five subjects you want to write about*. Look back over your other lists. There are the clues to what subjects you should write about. These lists allow you to direct your effort by helping you evaluate your personal experience, personal knowledge and personal interests.

Personal Experience

William Lederer, a successful nonfiction writer, once wrote: "Successful articles are usually built around ideas close to many readers, embracing their problems, ambitions and dreams." This understanding is vital when you're writing a personal experience story. We have all done things that live on in our minds. Perhaps it was a rafting adventure, meeting a famous person, an ordeal of survival or a family tragedy.

I can count several student writers in each of my classes who have lived through real-life dramas. They tell such stories as what it was like to be swept away in raging flood waters, clinging to a log for survival, or to be brutally beaten and left in a ditch to die. Others have written about their intense struggles with life-threatening diseases.

But your experience doesn't have to be sensational to sell. It may be a unique travel adventure, a special family event, a satisfying learning experience. However, a common mistake for beginning writers is thinking that *all* their life experiences are interesting to other people. Let's face it, a daily journal about a station wagon trip to the Ozark Mountains with your husband, Earl, the two kids, Jenny and Jud, and your sheepdog, Wooly, isn't likely to generate much interest. Unless you and Wooly fought off a grizzly bear barehanded, or Jenny and Jud saved a wounded deer from a mob of kill-crazed hunters, there's not much to recommend the story.

Before you write a personal experience story, ask yourself this: Would someone else want to read this? Then put yourself in the place of the reader and ask: Would I want to read this?

Here's a short personal experience story that I wrote because I felt others would enjoy reading it:

In the early 1970s, the cocktail bar at the Continental Hotel in Naples, Italy, was a lively meeting place for Americans living there.

One day, I was joined by a tweedy gentleman who shared my taste for the Continental's martinis. As we talked, I discovered he was also a writer whose fascination with the theater was equal to mine.

I mentioned that I dabbled in play production and hoped someday to direct the American classic, *Our Town*, by Thornton Wilder.

"Do you know the play?" I asked.

"My favorite," he replied.

"Difficult to do well," I said.

"Rarely done right," he agreed.

Then, grabbing a piece of paper from the bar, he began scribbling rapidly. Finished, he handed me the note, saying, "You might try it this way."

The note said:

Our Town *should be played without sentimentality
or ponderousness—simply, dryly and sincerely.*
                Sez

                old

                        *Thornton Wilder
                        Naples, Feb. 9, 1971*

This personal experience anecdote sold to *Reader's Digest*.

The nice thing about writing a personal experience story is that your research can be minimal—*you* are the expert. The story is about you.

My own experiences inspired most of the articles I wrote at the beginning of my writing career. I kept asking myself what experiences I could share. My story, "The TV Games People Play," centered on becoming a game-show contestant and sold to *The Saturday Evening Post*. The slant of the article was what it takes to get on a game show. Here's an excerpt from the article:

> Outside, the sun burned through the yellow haze and onto Hollywood's metropolitan grill. Inside, the sign on the door said "Heater-Quigley Productions." I took a deep breath and walked in.
>
> The fuzzy-haired secretary behind the desk said, "Hi. Here for *High Rollers?*" I grinned inanely, and she passed me an application form and pulled out a Polaroid camera. "Smile and say *greed*," she said.
>
> I put on my best homemade-jam smile and the flash went off.

From that opening scene, the reader shares the experience, reading over the writer's shoulder as the process of getting on a television game show is revealed.

You say you have never had anything fascinating happen to you? Don't be dismayed—write an article about *another person's experience*. You may know someone who has had an unusual adventure, has overcome a shattering illness, has won a million-dollar lottery or has done something unique or extraordinary. You can ghost-write the story under that person's name (with their approval, of course) or report on it in the third person under your own name.

A writer in my class had a friend who posed in dress store windows as a mannequin. Reactions by shoppers to the immobile "dummy" were unusual and varied. Two women tried to remove the model's blouse and try it on while others stared, trying to figure out if the mannequin was real. One unsuspecting girl slapped a wad of bubble gum on the model's elbow. Intrigued by these anecdotes, the writer put together an article on her friend's mannequin experiences.

Personal Knowledge

Writing from your personal knowledge, your area of expertise, is the best way to develop writing that will sell. Everyone knows how to do something as well as or better than someone else. That knowledge is saleable. The difficulty lies in recognizing that what you know is marketable.

One man in my writing class confessed after several sessions that he didn't have anything to write about. I asked him what he did for a living.

"I'm a mason," he answered, showing me his hands, which were rough and deeply etched with cracks, the fingernails jagged and unkempt. "I build stone walls, patios and sidewalks." He shrugged. "Nothing much to write about."

"Why don't you write an article on how to build a brick sidewalk," I suggested.

"Who'd want to read that?"

With a little more encouragement he wrote a rough draft and read it in class. He had even scratched out several pencil illustrations. After rewriting the piece he sent it off to *Popular Me-*

chanics. It sold for $350! The magazine's staff artist created the illustrations from the writer's rough drawings.

Why did this article sell? The writer had knowledge he could share with the reader.

A student writer who owned a bridal shop and specialized in making arrangements for weddings, queried *Bride's* magazine about a wedding article idea. The editor immediately responded with an assignment to write the article specifying a fee for the finished manuscript, the number of words required, and the issue of the magazine in which the article would appear. The student had *never written* an article before! But she had something the editor wanted—knowledge. This writer went on to do a series of articles for *Bride's* magazine.

Personal Interest

Following a personal interest allows you to break the rule, "write what you know," and write about something you *want* to know. We all want to learn something new: the French language, how to build a fiberglass boat or make handsome jewelry. Perhaps you've always been an armchair traveler but in retirement you suddenly have the time for *real* adventure.

In my early writing career, I thought all I ever wanted to do was write travel articles. But in my wanderings I discovered I was talking to a lot of people: shopkeepers, hotel owners, restaurant chefs. I enjoyed asking the questions and was most often intrigued by the answers. I began interviewing wine makers, theatrical directors and producers and finally famous movie stars, authors, composers, comedians. My interests as a writer had evolved and propelled me into writing the personality profile.

My writing students have also discovered new interests that have spawned articles. One older woman bought a word processor, took a course on operating the machine, and wrote an article titled, "Computer Granny," which she sold to a Christian magazine. A male writer took a microwave oven cooking class through a local adult education program and discovered he was the only man in the class. He wrote a clever story on his class cooking experiences titled, "Microman!"

News and Magazine Items

It's not just our personal experience, knowledge and interests that can inspire us with article ideas. Writers must also be voracious readers. What we glean from newspapers and magazine items can spawn saleable stories, as well.

Remember the *Jaws* craze? The press inundated the public with shark stories. One enterprising student writer read in a southern California newspaper that a swimmer had been attacked and severely injured by a shark at a nearby beach. The writer grabbed a pen and notebook, went to the hospital where the man was recovering, interviewed him, quickly wrote the story, and sent it off to *Saga* magazine. One week later the writer got a phone call from the editor. The magazine was replacing the cover of the next issue and running the shark story as its feature piece! One month later, there it was, a close-up photograph of a white shark on the cover, its massive mouthful of jagged teeth ready to rip through the page. The headline read: SWIMMER ATTACKED BY MAN-EATING SHARK!

Here's an even bigger headline story that appeared in newspapers across the country many years ago:

TEXAS "CHICKEN RANCH" CLOSES AFTER 129 YEARS

LA GRANGE, TEX.—A Central Texas ranch which served as a bawdy house for six generations turned out its red light and the ladies who called the house a home packed their bags and headed for other jobs.

One enterprising freelancer, recognizing the story value of the "Chicken Ranch," wrote an article on the subject and sold it to

Playboy. The story was eventually made into the hit Broadway musical, *The Best Little Whorehouse in Texas*.

The best newspapers in which to uncover ideas are regional journals or hometown newspapers. Look for items that are not written by syndicates like King Features or wire services like AP or UPI. Remember, you are not the only writer looking at news items and trying to discover gold in black and white. A local item like the shark story can have great national appeal.

Make reading a newspaper or magazine a treasure hunt. When you see something that interests you, clip the piece out and save it. Start files on different subjects. You will soon have enough research material to write your story.

I once cut out a short piece from *Parade* magazine that told the story of two Oxford students who had sent author Rudyard Kipling ten shillings with a note that said, "We understand you get ten shillings for each word you write. Find enclosed ten shillings for one word."

Kipling responded with the word, "Thanks."

The anecdote was clever and I saved it. About a month later I bought a book called *The Address Book: How to Reach Anyone Who's Anyone*. As I was thumbing its pages I noticed such names as Norman Mailer, Sidney Sheldon, Mario Puzo, William F. Buckley, Jr., Judith Krantz—then I recognized an idea. What if I sent letters to these famous writers asking for one word? Would any of these authors respond? If enough did, I could collect them into a "roundup" article and sell it. (Roundups ask questions of celebrities, such as, "What was your best Christmas present?" or "What is your favorite book?") I sent a letter to thirty writers, enclosed a crisp new one dollar bill and a note that said, "I understand you get a dollar a word for your writing. Please find enclosed a dollar in payment for one word."

To my surprise, most of the authors responded. The first to do so was syndicated columnist Art Buchwald. On his letterhead he typed: LOVE

The erudite and usually verbose William F. Buckley, Jr., who must have struggled to keep to the one-word limit, responded with the scribbled reply: HI!

Robert Ludlum, who dreams up spy thrillers, sent the dollar back with this handwritten memo that illustrates his investigative insight:

> I was going to write THANKS and keep the buck! However, upon close examination I've come to the conclusion that it [the dollar] is entirely too clean, bright and pressed to be authentic and therefore have concluded that you wish to put me in jail for passing counterfeit money.
> Nice try, pal.

Norman Mailer sent two dollars back, adding a typed note that read: "You get my silver-dollar word. It is: EXCELSIOR. (And receive two dollars in return for the most original letter of the month.)"

Leon Uris replied: SHALOM. He added, "You made my day."

Alex Haley sent an autographed photo that said, "To Cork Millner, with best wishes to you, my colleague." He added a note, "You can send the money for those twelve words later."

PNEUMOCOCCUS came from Isaac Asimov; RATS from "Peanuts" cartoonist, Charles Schulz. Ray Bradbury, Mario Puzo, Sidney Sheldon, Gay Talese, and Edward Albee mirrored Kipling's reply by writing THANKS or THANK YOU. Judith Krantz wrote, THANKS, but added, "This is the first tax-free dollar I have ever earned. I shall treasure it!"

The article, "The Buck Stops Here," was printed in the *Los Angeles Times Magazine*, then picked up as a reprint by several magazines and finally syndicated to a hundred newspapers. Yes, it pays to read newspapers and magazines and clip items of interest.

You may also get ideas from the books you read. I bought Robert Fulghum's charming collection of uncommon thoughts on common things, *All I Really Need to Know I Learned in Kinder-*

garten. He listed, as he said, "things I don't understand." Many of them could work as ideas for magazine articles:

"Is the recent marketing of cologne for dogs a sign of anything?" (An idea for a dog-grooming article.)

"Why can't we just spell it 'orderves' and get it over with?" (Perhaps an article on word-derivation.)

"Why aren't there any traditional Halloween carols?" (An idea for a seasonal article on Halloween.)

Put your own imagination to work on these:

"Why do people drop a letter in the mailbox and then open the lid again to see if it really went down?"

"Why are there zebras?"

Ideas the Reader Can Relate To

Why are Erma Bombeck and Andy Rooney successful? Because they are funny? Try again. Their clever way of writing? Nope. Their ability to write about everyday items? You're close. Both humorists write columns about things their audience can *relate to*. They write about junk mail, garage sales, coupon collecting, health foods, dieting fads: things that readers are aquainted with or have suffered through themselves.

I've had students write on such everyday topics as talking cash registers, taking the kids to fast-food restaurants, and grocery store carts. Grocery store carts! Why would anyone want to write about grocery store carts? Doesn't it always seem when you go to a store you have to tug and yank to get two carts apart, then the one you get has a wheel that chatters and steers you into a stack of cans? Ever drive off with another shopper's cart, or turn away for an instant and find yours gone? There isn't a person in the United States who hasn't pushed a grocery cart. Readers relate instantly to this universal subject.

Compelling Categories

There are several categories of article subjects that reliably arouse an editor's attention. They are:

- How-to articles
- Seasonal subjects
- Timely items
- Self-help stories

HOW-TO ARTICLES

A "how-to" is exactly what it sounds like: an article that tells readers how to do something: "How to Build a Family Room," "How to Plant a Rose Garden," "How to Dress Thin."

How-to articles are hot—and always have been—and are purchased by the thousands each month by editors looking for ideas to keep their readers reading. Almost anything you do can be turned into a how-to article. Perhaps you collect buttons, create wall hangings, install carpets, build cabinets. Editors know that their readers are always interested in learning new skills, techniques, or shortcuts. All you have to do is transform your expertise into a well-organized, step-by-step set of instructions.

SEASONAL SUBJECTS

Do you have a Christmas story idea? Perhaps you know a different way to hide Easter eggs. Do you have a special story about Mother's Day? Independence Day? Father's Day? National Garlic Day? Remember to submit seasonal articles early—at least six months *before* the holiday because editors have to plan their issues six to eight months in advance.

One student writer wrote a short personal story titled, "Watching," about observing her twelve-year-old daughter grow up. *Ladies' Home Journal* bought this poignant first-person piece for their Mother's Day issue.

TIMELY SUBJECTS

Be careful with this one. By the time you recognize a trend, the magazine's staff has probably already thought of it and assigned a writer to do the story. Avoid the topics that are on everyone's lips. If you discover something that is genuinely new, then write about it.

A student once told me she was going to do an article on the Rubik Cube. At the time, almost everyone had bought and toyed with a Rubik cube puzzle, so I asked her if she had a different slant.

"Got a great one!" she answered, smiling confidently.

The next week she came in with an article titled, "The Rubik Cube Cake." She had baked a cake using different colors of icing for the cubes and defined the lines with strips of black licorice. It was a timely *recipe*.

SELF-HELP

Editors know that readers want to enhance the quality of their lives: to lose thirty pounds, succeed in business, be a better homemaker, improve their relationship within their husband or wife. This craving for self-improvement is marketable—if you can offer practical advice. Whenever a licensed therapist, such as a marriage counselor, attends my writing class, I can almost guarantee that that writer will sell a self-help magazine article. Writing a clear, easily understood article in one of the four categories mentioned above will improve your chances of selling what you write.

By building your own idea factory and using the results intelligently you can insure a steady flow of saleable manuscripts. Before you know it, instead of saying, "What can I write about?"

you'll be saying, "Which idea will I *select* to write about next?" You'll soon have too many ideas—more than you'll ever be able to get onto paper. And they'll be new, fresh, better ideas—saleable ideas.

That idea you originally got from the magazine in the dentist's office might lead to a sale—and even pay for your gold filling!

2
The Craft

OF WRITING NONFICTION

Writing Great Leads

Easy reading is damned hard writing.
—Nathaniel Hawthorne

ctor David Niven wanted to write a book. There was just one problem: Niven had no idea *how* to write a book. So he did what any fledgling writer would do: he asked for advice from an established writer, in this case a well-known author. The author replied, "It must have a beginning, middle and end."

Overly simplistic? Hardly. Niven used the advice and went on to write the bestseller, *The Moon's a Balloon*.

Let's take a closer look at this beginning, middle and end by taking a 2,500-word article and breaking it down into a simple structure. Most magazines use articles varying in length from 800 to 1,800 words, with 2,500 words being the standard for feature-length articles. There are exceptions: *Vanity Fair, The New Yorker*, and *Playboy*, to name a few, use articles 3,000 to 6,000 words long.

Here's how the word count on a typical 2,500-word article would be broken down:

Beginning	Middle	End
25–250 words	2,000 + words	25–250 words

The most important words—those first 25 to 250 words—are the beginning, or what magazine editors call the "lead."

The Lead

The purpose of the lead is not only to catch the eye of the eventual reader, but to spark the interest of the editor you are trying to sell. To do that you must grab the editor's attention and interest immediately—or face a fast rejection. *Think of the lead as a sales pitch that plugs your product.* It is a promise to the editor that if he buys your product readers will buy his magazine.

I once invited an editor I had worked with for several years to lunch. Arriving at his office a few minutes early, I found him huddled over his desk, reading a stack of manuscripts.

"I'll be with you in a few minutes," he said, thumbing the manuscripts. "I've just got to read these submissions."

"But that will take hours," I said, thinking of my stomach.

"Give me ten minutes. Most of this stuff is going to be unreadable. I can tell by the lead whether I will accept it or not."

This editor is not alone in stressing the importance of a good lead. "If the first words don't grab me," another editor told me, "then I know the article won't satisfy my readers, so I pass it by in a hurry."

Not fair? Hardly. If the writer can't keep the editor reading from the opening lines to the last sentence, the writer had better think about making some improvements.

How many times have you picked up a magazine, thumbed through the pages, stopped when the subject of an article got your interest, and begun to read? And how many times have you lost interest within the first few paragraphs and flipped through the pages to another article? The reason you stopped reading was not because the subject matter didn't intrigue you. You quit because the writer was not able to gain and sustain your interest. When you turned to another article you were, in effect, acting like an editor—you were rejecting the article.

Don McKinney, onetime editor of *McCall's*, once wrote a magazine article titled, "How to Write an Article Lead." In doing so, McKinney put himself on the spot. With that title, the article lead had to be good. What did McKinney do? He began the article with a quote from an article he had once accepted for publication in *McCall's:*

> She is sitting alone in the crumb-strewn kitchen, clutching
> a yellow coffee cup in her quivering hands and thinking of
> ways to kill her husband.

Good lead—or bad? Was McKinney trying to fool the reader? Here's how he continued:

> As article leads go, that is right in there with, " 'Take your
> hand off my knee!' cried the duchess," the all-time cliché
> example of a successful way of catching the reader's at-
> tention.

Frankly, the lead may have worked as an attention-grabber, but the adjective-laden prose deserved some editing.

Let's break a lead's first 25 to 250 attention-getting words into two elements: the *hook* and the *slant*.

How the Hook Works

Editors use the term *hook* when referring to capturing the reader's attention. It's like hooking a fish and reeling it in.

> As she stepped into the bathtub with a glass of champagne
> and her best friend's husband, the doorbell rang.

Now that hook is startling enough to keep any reader awake. Who's at that door!

Here's another, similar hook:

> The last man on Earth sat alone in a room. Then he heard a knock at the door . . .

Both of these hooks pull the reader into the story, promising that something spectacular is going to happen in the next paragraph or the next few pages. In the first case, the reader asks, Who's at the door? The best friend? Or someone else? In the second case, is the knock from an alien who has conquered Earth and imprisoned the last man? Or is it the last *woman* on Earth? Or . . . what . . . ?

After you write your hook, reread it carefully, objectively—as if through the editor's eyes. If your writing does not reach out and grab the reader by the scruff of the neck and throw him into the paragraphs that follow, then rewrite the hook until it does.

Hook-Writing Techniques

Here are more detailed techniques that can be used to snag the reader:

- Narrative
- Creating a scene
- Character, action and dialogue
- Anecdotes
- Quotes
- Surprise or suspense
- Questions
- Imagery
- Atmosphere

NARRATIVE

Most magazine articles are written in the narrative form for two simple reasons:

1. They are the easiest to write.

2. They are always in demand.

The narrative style can work for you if your writing is complete, readable and as interesting as possible. Unfortunately, too much narrative writing is dull. Here's a lead from a recent article that appeared in *Westways* magazine:

> The Lower Canyons region of the Rio Grande is a 94-mile portion of the river that begins at the eastern boundary of Big Bend National Park and ends near Dryden, Texas.

Here's another that appeared in the same issue:

> A rough dirt road leisurely follows the contours of Lake Kerkinitis in northern Greece, giving the visitor time to admire the vista of dark blue water.

You decide whether either of these two "grabbers" makes you want to read on. To me they're both pretty dull.

There is nothing wrong with using narrative prose—if the writing gets the reader's attention. Here is the lead from a travel article I wrote titled, "Spain's Paradores—The Inn Places to Stay," that works much better:

> If you are the type of traveler who, along with Conrad Hilton, likes to collect hotels, to be engulfed in their atmosphere and discover the little secrets about them, to love them and savor their food, then Spain's National Tourist Inns—the *paradores*—are for you. For those that follow the "parador route"—a yearly pilgrimage to the different government-run accommodations—collecting a one night's stay in a parador is like saving bubble gum cards.

Now let's carry the prose narrative a step further by adding dramatic action to the writing equation. The following is taken from a story

I wrote called "Howard Hughes and the Spruce Goose," and chronicles the day in 1947 when the millionaire aviator flew his 400,000-pound flying boat, nicknamed the "Spruce Goose," seventy feet into the air.

> Howard Hughes eased his lean frame onto the seat behind the pilot's console, took off his favorite brown fedora and put on earphones. As he grasped the throttles that controlled the huge flying boat's eight engines, he smiled. *Today is the day*, the smile said—*today is the day!*

Many beginning writers think that narrative prose is the *only* way to begin an article. I did. Here's an example of early writing from my own files in an article called, "Guadalupe: A Medieval Village and Its Mysterious Virgin," which appeared in *Diversion* magazine:

> Guadalupe, Spain, is a medieval community in working order. The rough, narrow, cobblestone streets that twist up and down the hills of the village are stacked with tattered cottages that could have welcomed a serf many centuries ago. Crumbling balconies blossom with begonias, and the smell of hot olive oil and sour wine drifts from doorways. The people are cheerful and contented, living on terms of friendship with the hens, pigs, and cows that inhabit the cottages with them.

"Blossom with begonias . . . *drifts from doorways!"* Sigh. I worked *so* hard to make those sentences sound literary. I labored over them—then happened upon something quite by accident in the next paragraphs. I created a scene that had character, action and dialogue—and it was *easy* to write:

> Near the center of the village an old woman dressed in black leads an ancient burro up the street. A tourist raises his camera and photographs the scene. The woman stops.

She watches him with the look of the very old who stare as if their eyes could wipe away the mystery of the object and reveal its true nature.

Then she says in Spanish, "You take the picture of my donkey, but not of me. Am I not near so pretty?" A smile creases her dry skin and the tourist takes the picture.

"*Gracias, Vieja*" (Thanks, old one), he says.

"*Vaya con Dios*" (Go with God), she replies, a farewell that is used only by the old in Spain today. She pulls the donkey's rope and struggles up the street to the center of the village where a rose-colored church casts its massive shadow over a fountain. The old brass doors, which creak more agonizingly than most in Spain, are worn smooth where pressed by thousands of hands who have come to see the miraculous statue of the Virgin Mary—Our Lady of Guadalupe. The statue is the reason for the village's existence.

This scene with the old woman and her donkey is alive, readable and, most of all, visual. The scene also leads into what the story is all about—the mysterious statue of the Virgin Mary which was said to have been carved by Saint Paul.

CREATING A SCENE

A scene adds a fictionlike touch to any nonfiction story. Here's an example of a profile that appeared in *The Saturday Evening Post* on actor Jimmy Stewart, titled, "Ah . . . Waal . . . Here's Jimmy Stewart."

It is early afternoon as I walk up to Jimmy Stewart's Tudor-style home in Beverly Hills. A small van crammed with tourists on a "See the Stars' Homes!" tour quickly comes to a stop in the street. They press their noses against the van's windows and wait expectantly. I ring the bell.

The door opens and Jimmy Stewart stands framed in

the entryway looking as if he had stepped out of a vintage Norman Rockwell painting. His gangling 6-foot-3½-inch frame is attired in a blue blazer, gray slacks and a maroon tie; he blends perfectly with the Ivy League feel of the brick house. Stewart shakes my hand, then, seeing the bus, waves at the tourists.

"You . . . ah . . . waal . . . you'd better wave," he says in the world's most imitated voice. I wave. Jimmy waves. The film fans grin wildly and wave back, their shouts of "Hi, Jimmy!" muffled by the sealed windows of the van.

"Well now . . . come on . . . come on in," Jimmy Stewart says. He waves one last time then closes the door behind us.

See how it works! In this example, the present tense is used, putting the reader into the scene, allowing him to walk into Jimmy Stewart's house with the writer.

CHARACTER, ACTION AND DIALOGUE

Action doesn't mean knock-down-drag-out brawls, or flaming car crashes; action can be two people walking on a beach or sitting down to a quiet lunch. Here's a scene using character, action and dialogue. Titled "My Wife the Animalholic," by student writer King Harris, it appeared in *The Saturday Evening Post*.

Fear bubbled in my stomach as the horseman galloped by and roared at me, "Tell your wife to shut up, or I'll ram your teeth down your throat."

He veered away from us and threw up a cloud of dust, as my wife shouted at him:

"If you beat that animal one more time, I'm calling the humane society! Don't you know you can't control a horse with brute strength?" Cupping her hands around her mouth, she yelled, "When knowledge ends, violence takes over!" Then she looked at me to *do* Something.

Pretty lively stuff! Note how vivid the scene becomes with the use of character, action and dialogue. In the scene, which begins at a moment of high drama, we can "see" the action, and picture the three characters. The quotation marks in the dialogue also catch the eye of the reader.

ANECDOTES

Anecdotes are little stories within a story and, as such, have a beginning, middle and end. Anecdotes are the pictures that go along with ideas. They put flesh on the bones of your article.

Here's an example of using an anecdote. It was taken from a personality profile of Dame Judith Anderson, the dramatic actress knighted by Queen Elizabeth II:

> Dame Judith Anderson is standing on the edge of the movie set between takes while the cameras and lighting equipment are being reset. An electrician on a ladder yells down to her: "Hey, Judy, baby, move over a few feet!"
>
> The great dramatic actress slowly swivels her head upward and in her deep resonant voice says, "It's *Dame* Judy Baby!"

Want to read another anecdote? Check the David Niven lead to *this* chapter.

QUOTES

"Frankly, my dear, I don't give a damn."

By using this familiar line, the writer has caught our attention. It has impact because we didn't expect it and wonder how it ties in with the article. (In this case, the piece was about communication and angry, walk-out-the-door scenes in marriages.)

How about this one?

I see, Kiwi,
You have wings
But cannot fly.
Yes, that is true
But . . . what do you do?
Everything else.

—Old Japanese poem

This poem was the lead to a story about a theatre for the handicapped. Quotations from poetry or famous works of writing, such as the Bible or Shakespeare, can serve as effective transitions into the story.

Quotes from a prominent or outspoken person can also attract the reader's attention and add vitality and credibility to a manuscript. Here's a lead from an article on TV game shows using quotes from a well-known person:

"What kind of contestant are we looking for? It takes a type," says Mark Goodson, TV's godfather of game shows. "We want hype and we want enthusiasm, personality and a little reasoning ability. And you can't fake it. It has to be there!"

SURPRISE OR SUSPENSE

The "Greatest Show on Earth" is shrinking!

Surprised? This short hook was from a story on the Ringling Brothers and Barnum & Bailey Circus. How about this shocker:

John Fulton, America's premier matador, is alive and well and living in Seville, Spain—and painting in blood.

A matador painting in blood! The lead startles, or astonishes, or shocks the reader. When it works, the reader must read on. (In this case, the story went on to tell how Fulton, a former art student and bullfighter, paints pictures of bulls in bull's blood. He says, "The only pigment I use in my paintings comes from the bulls I have fought and killed in the arena.")

Here's another shocker. It's the lead from a story in the book *Tug-O'-War*, by student writer Russ Reina, which couples the techniques of creating a scene with a startling hook:

> "Here," I said. "Let me show you."
>
> I leaned over the ambulance stretcher and gingerly took the woman's right forearm in my hands, taking care not to disturb the IV. The sleeve of her light cotton pajama top was already rolled above her elbow.
>
> "Next time," I continued, "pull the telephone cord out of the wall. Then, if you're serious, take the razor blade and slice *down* the vein, not across."

The writer, a paramedic, was trying to find a way to deal with a woman who had tried several times to commit suicide.

And suspense? This nine-word hook from "Montraldo" by John Cheever promises a lot more to come:

> The first time I robbed Tiffany's, it was raining.

QUESTIONS

Posing a question can titillate or challenge a reader. The trick of asking a question to hook the reader has been around for a long time, but it still works:

> How would you like to write a best-seller?

> Did you know you can make $20,000 a year writing greeting cards?

> How would you like to make a million bucks and see the world for free as a travel agent?

IMAGERY

> The fiery golden sunset was a pleasant memory in Janet's mind as dusk settled on the roadway and the white glare of headlights flickered in the oncoming traffic. She touched the blinker signal and pulled up to the red light. As the light turned green and she stepped on the accelerator, a dark sedan appeared out of nowhere, and went zooming around the corner.

This lead, from an article titled, "The Color of Your Life," by student writer Jo Anne Heuston appeared in *Consumer Life* magazine and uses imagery to hook the reader. The reader can "see" the incident at the stoplight and wants to know what happened next.

Here's the beginning of "The Angel of the Bridge" by John Cheever that creates a charming picture:

> You may have seen my mother waltzing on ice skates in Rockefeller Center. She's very wiry, and she wears a red velvet costume with a short skirt.

ATMOSPHERE

> It was a dark and stormy night . . .

That hook—even more than the fairy-tale beginning, "Once upon a time . . ."—is the most famous opening line in writing. Where did it originate? "Peanuts" cartoonist Charles Schulz, who has Snoopy write the line, has no idea where the phrase came from. "It's just one of the phrases or words I like my characters to say," Schulz says, "like 'Good Grief' or 'Rats.' " (In fact, "It was a dark and stormy night . . ." first appeared in 1830 as the opening sentence of the novel *Paul Clifford* by Edward Bulwer-Lytton, a writer

better known for his dramatic potboiler, *The Last Days of Pompeii*.)
"Lashing rain." "Streaks of lightning split open the dark clouds." Such phrases create an atmosphere that entices the reader to keep turning pages. After all, nothing exciting happens on a bright, sunny day. But on a "dark and stormy night . . ." anything could happen.

The Slant

The second element of the lead is the *slant*—the article's *angle, focus,* or *point of view* on its subject.

You need a slant for the same reason you need a channel for irrigation water: to keep the liquid from uselessly draining away all over the place. A slant keeps your article pointed in the right direction. If readers cannot figure out what the article is about, they'll turn the page. The slant must be clearly stated. Here's an example of a complete lead from an article I wrote for *Overseas Family* magazine titled "Rodeo in Spain" that includes both a hook and a slant.

The gate on the number three chute flew open. A bull charged into the arena. The crowd gasped; the cowboys behind the chute leaned forward over the railing, their bodies moving instinctively with the gyrations of the man clinging desperately to the back of the bull.

"Throw him, Steel!" the cowboys yelled.

"Hook him, Jack!"

The center of their attention was a cowboy named "Jumping Jack" Welch who grimly held on to a rope wrapped around the twisting bull's middle. In his scarlet shirt and red-and-blue chaps he looked like a flapping butterfly pinned to the animal's back.

Jumping Jack Welch rides bulls and broncs on weekends. During the week he serves as a Navy deep-sea diver attached to the Naval Station at Rota, Spain. He is one of

the dozen sailors who temporarily shed their Navy careers
to bring the excitement of an American rodeo to Spain.

The last paragraph clearly states the slant. Everything up to that
point was a character, dialogue and action hook. What is the article
about? An American rodeo in Spain.

The slant may be very simple and straightforward. If you write
a piece about how to build a toolshed that begins, "This article
will show you how to build a toolshed," that's your slant. However,
the slant could be narrower in focus if the article was written with
the idea of building a toolshed to house garden equipment or
automobile repair tools.

Six Symptoms of Sick Leads

Recognize the telltale signs of creative disorder. Check whether
your lead:

1. Is too long for the rest of the article. Try to keep it to a
   manuscript page or less.
2. Fails to identify the slant.
3. Rambles, or is made up of sprawling sentences.
4. Contains pointless anecdotal material or quotes having
   nothing to do with the slant.
5. Uses obscure, pedantic prose.
6. Is boring.

Choosing the Lead

Determining the best lead for your article can be a devilish chore.
It is not uncommon for writers to agonize for hours over a lead,
only to discover that the first few paragraphs must be thrown away.
"How do I begin my article?" you wonder as you sit, hands poised,
over your computer keyboard. You can start by asking yourself
these questions:

1. What is the single most important thing I have to say in my article?
2. What is most interesting or the most astounding fact in the article?
3. What is there about my article that makes it different?

Your answers to those three questions will help you identify the lead.

A student once turned in a travel article that began something like this:

> Fred and I got up early, loaded the station wagon with camping equipment and shoved the two kids in the back seat. Then Fred turned on the ignition, put the car in reverse, backed out of the driveway and we were off to Alaska.

Well, unless Fred backs the station wagon into a circus truck loaded with snarling lions, nobody's going to read further. I asked what was the single most interesting thing this writer could remember about the trip to Alaska. "Oh, you'd never guess," she said, her eyes coming alive, "We saw palm trees in Alaska!" "Okay," I told her, "*that's* your hook. Now write it."

If you simply cannot think of a way to start your article, then begin by summing up what you want to say in a first paragraph. At least this will clarify the slant. Then write a rough draft of the complete article, not worrying about how you begin. Yes, you can even start with Fred backing the loaded station wagon out of the driveway. Once you're into the article, don't worry about how well it's going—just keep writing.

After you have finished the first rough draft, reread it and ask yourself these questions:

1. At what point did the writing come alive?
2. Was there some episode or fact that stated your slant perfectly?

3. Was there an attention-grabbing anecdote?
4. Did any scene stand out visually?
5. Did rereading the article remind you of a forgotten anecdote or fact that would make a great lead?

Even if you started with what you thought was the perfect lead, you may want to change it once you start writing. Many times I have found the hook to a student writer's article on page three. Page three! Why does the hook pop up on page three? The answer is simple: It takes a few pages for a writer to get rolling.

A good working knowledge of lead-writing techniques may not eliminate all your first-paragraph problems, but it will lessen the anguish when you face that blank paper.

Leads add excitement and readability to your articles. Avoid getting stuck in a rut—use several different techniques. Better yet, try them all. Writing a good lead is a critical step toward collecting your first byline.

Variety in Your Writing

I love being a writer. What I can't stand is the paperwork.

—Peter De Vries

You're in the dentist's office for a checkup. You pick up a magazine, thumb through the pages and come across an article that interests you enough to start reading. After a few minutes your mind wanders, and you have to reread paragraphs. Boring stuff. Your concentration trails off and you shake your head to get back on track. Nope, still boring. Like so many other articles you have read, this one can't maintain your interest. What went wrong? The idea was stimulating. The title was intriguing . . .

The problem was the middle. It was just plain dull.

Capturing the reader's attention with an exciting lead isn't enough. If you do not want your article to stimulate the yawn reflex, then you'll have to write with variety. Monotony in writing is like a paralyzing frost. The Greeks were aware of the value of variety and contrast: they set off the beauty of flowers by planting them next to onions and leeks.

Structure

Let's use a graph to analyze how an article should be structured. In the graph below the reader interest level is rated from zero to ten. The length of the article is 2,500 words, which is the average length of a feature piece in a major magazine.

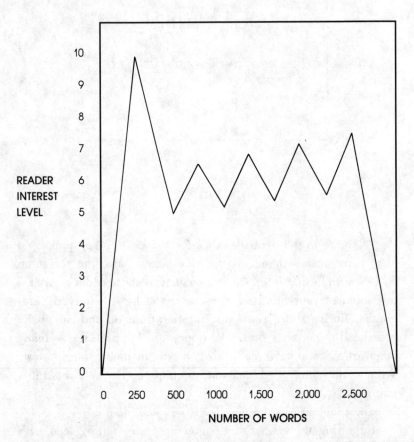

Note that in this case reader interest peaks at the hook, those first 25 to 250 words. And it should, because the hook should include the most fascinating thing you have to say about your subject. Obviously, it is impossible to sustain a level that high throughout 2,500 words. You also will have to present the background, historical or expository material that is necessary to round out your article. Unfortunately, that material is probably less interesting. Each time the interest level dips, you are in danger of losing your readers. If it hits zero, readers will turn to the next article. How to recapture their interest? By varying the way you present your material.

Variety

Let's make this easy. Remember what I told you in the previous chapter about writing great leads? Rebuild interest in the "body" of your material by returning to six of the same nine techniques you used to create a compelling lead. These techniques are the ones used most commonly:

- Narrative
- Anecdotes
- Quotes
- Imagery
- Creating a scene
- Character, action and dialogue

A mix of these attention-grabbing elements throughout the article will add that needed variety—and readability.

A Writing Recipe

Like a master chef, you can spice up your writing recipe by adding unusual ingredients: a pinch of dialogue, a teaspoonful of quotes, a dash of anecdotes. To understand how this writing recipe works, let's analyze a 2,500-word article, "Devil's Island: 'The Green Hell,' " that was published in *Islands* magazine.

I had visited the infamous penal colony off French Guiana and was shocked by the number of prisoners—70,000—who had been incarcerated there in the hundred years it was in operation (from

1848 to the late 1940s) and by how many had died during their imprisonment—approximately 50,000. I was struck by the brutality of the place. But there was something more, something I couldn't put my finger on at first, something unusual . . .

Walking around Île Royale, one of the three tiny islands that make up the offshore portion of the penal colony, I was amazed to see that most of the old stone cells and buildings had turned to rubble. Nothing could account for the destruction; there had not been an earthquake, typhoon or volcanic upheaval. Then it came to me. Of course! The *ghosts* of the prisoners were destroying the terrible place stone by stone. Although brutality was the predominant theme, the slant of the article, ghosts, became the thread that held the story together.

Here are some excerpts from the Devil's Island article I wrote and an analysis of the various techniques I used to maintain reader interest.

Devil's Island: "The Green Hell"
by Cork Millner

"*Oui monsieur*, the sound . . . it is the ghosts of the prisoners, the *bagnards* . . . they brush against the trees in anguish." The old Frenchman whispered the last word, "anguish," as he listened to the sighing of the palm trees.

"It is only the breeze from the ocean," I shrugged, not quite sure. There was a disturbing rustle of palm fronds.

The Frenchman pouted, shook his head slowly, then with heavy accent added, "No, *monsieur*, today the heat is heavy with them. In the air you can feel the weight of generations of *bagnards*. They are still here, imprisoned in the green hell of *l'Île du Diable*—imprisoned on Devil's Island."

That is the *hook*. Note how *character, action and dialogue* are used to stimulate the interest and establish the ghosts concept. The Frenchman is *fiction*. Although there was a French caretaker on the island, he spoke only French, and I only English, therefore the dialogue, as written, did not take place. Used wisely, a certain amount of "fictional truth" can improve a piece of nonfiction. However, quotes should not be made up that lead the reader away from the facts of the story.

> Devil's Island. The sound of the name sent a shiver through me. For Devil's Island, a steamy speck of land off the coast of French Guiana just above the shoulder of Brazil, was the most infamous of the twentieth century's penal colonies. Today its lush tropical foliage, deepened by the intensity of the equatorial sun, easily belies its brutal past. It has the strange aura of a paradise lost.

The above paragraph is background *narrative* written to establish the island's location. The article goes on for another 300 words telling about the origin of the penal colony, when the French established it, how many prisoners were incarcerated there, how they were buried at sea without ceremony, and when the prison was closed. (Note: The article could have begun with the line: "Devil's Island. The sound of the name sent a shiver through me . . ." Nothing wrong with that lead, but in this case *character, action and dialogue* work better to hook the reader.) At this point the narrative has continued for over 400 words. Although necessary background information has been introduced, the reader's interest could be waning. It's time to toss other ingredients into the recipe: *character, action and dialogue*.

> The old Frenchman, a gray beret pulled tightly to his eyebrows, met me when I stepped onto the dock at Royale. The husk of a dead cigarette hung in the corner of his

mouth, and his right eye, constantly wary from decades of
curling smoke, was squeezed to a slit.

When introducing a character into short nonfiction, it is best to
give a *brief* description. Just enough to give the reader a quick
visual *image:* "He was a fireplug of a man," or "He looked like a
German beer hall tuba player."

"Welcome to *l'Île Royale, Monsieur*," he said, flipping the
blackened cigarette into the sea. A whisper of air rushed
through the palm trees and the Frenchman squinted sus-
piciously at the rustling leaves for a moment. He shrugged,
then turned back to me and nodded to the neighboring
island. "Saint Joseph. The *bagnards* called it *la mangeuse
d'hommes*, the devourer of men. On the island there was
a special prison called the *Reclusion*. It was the place of
solitary confinement. Few survived."

   "And Devil's Island?" I asked. I had yet to see the
island, hidden from view by the 500-foot-high plateau of
Royale.

   "Ah, *l'Île du Diable*," he sighed. "The *bagnards*
called it the dry guillotine. Fewer survived on Devil's Island."

Most of the information in the above dialogue is expository material,
all of which could have been done in *narrative*. A mixture of
dialogue and narrative can make information more palatable. I
found very little research material on Devil's Island. One of the
books I used was *Papillon* by Henri Charriere, a fascinating story
about a prisoner's life on the island. The following *quote* not only
shows the brutality of life in the penal colony, but is also strikingly
visual.

In his autobiography, Papillon, the celebrated inmate who
spent twelve years imprisoned on the islands and escaped

to tell about it, described the burial of a fellow prisoner, a close friend named Matthieu: "Wrapped in flour sacks, Matthieu's body slid from the small boat into the water. Jesus! He was no sooner in the water—for good, I thought—than he rose above the surface, lifted by, I don't know, seven, ten, maybe twenty sharks. The flour sacks were torn off, and for perhaps two or three seconds Matthieu seemed to be literally standing on the water. His right forearm was already gone. With half his body out of the water he was bearing down on our boat when an eddy caught him and he disappeared. . . . Everybody, guards included, was terror-stricken."

Well, enough of the macabre. It's time to get back to the Frenchman. We still have Devil's Island to see.

The Frenchman dug into his pants pocket and pulled out a crumpled pack of cigarettes as wrinkled as his face. He plucked a shriveled black cigarette from the pack, wet the end with his lips and stuck it into the corner of his mouth. The right eye squeezed tight as he pulled out a match. "Only Papillon escaped the sharks." The match flared.

Note how visual elements—*imagery*—are used in the dialogue. The use of imagery allows the reader to step into the picture. The Frenchman now becomes my guide, taking me around the island, pointing out crumbling ruins of cell blocks, the encroaching jungle of palms and vines—and finally, Devil's Island.

We rounded a rock promontory, and the easterly sea breeze blew suddenly crisp, fresh and cool in our faces, a relief from the penetrating heat and stillness of the air on the leeward side of the island.

"There!" he shouted above the crashing waves. "There—*l'Île du Diable!*"

Devil's Island was suddenly, startlingly close, not much more than a stone's throw from where we stood on the beach. It looked like a miniature tropical paradise, a peaceful island less than a mile in length and a few hundred yards wide, shaped like a thick baseball bat. Only a few decaying red brick huts, engulfed by an undergrowth of palm trees, recalled the island's past as a maximum security prison. Waves crashed relentlessly on the rocky shores as if trying to wash away a century of brutality and suffering.

The reader has now seen the island. But what more can we describe? You can only say so much about swaying palm trees and crashing waves. We need to know *what happened* on the island. One of the few books I found in English was the diary of one of the famous political prisoners who had been imprisoned there in 1894, Captain Dreyfus. A good *quote* from that diary would *show* what the island was like.

On the second night on the island, Dreyfus rose from his cot, and by the light of the prison guard's lantern started a diary:

"It is impossible for me to sleep. This cage before which the guard walks up and down like a phantom appearing in my dreams, the plague of insects which run over my skin, the rage that is smothered in my heart that I should be here, when I have always and everywhere done my duty—all this overexcites my nerves which are already shattered and drives away sleep. . . ."

Well, now that we've put this innocent man on this miserable island, we've got to finish his story and get him off. The *narrative* continues:

> In 1898, after Dreyfus had been imprisoned four years, another officer was accused, and acquitted, of Dreyfus's alleged crime. At a court-martial in 1899, Dreyfus—by then a broken man with white hair and stuttering speech— was again convicted. Still proclaiming his innocence, Dreyfus accepted a government pardon. He was not fully exonerated until 1906, whereupon he was awarded the Legion of Honor medal and reinstatement in the army. Regaining his health, he served gallantly in World War I and died in 1935, a quiet old gentleman who kept tightly locked within his soul the burning memory of Devil's Island.
>
> "There is a stone bench on the far shore of the island where Monsieur Dreyfus would sit and gaze out to sea, toward France and his family." The old Frenchman pointed to the opposite end of Devil's Island. "It is the same stone bench where Papillon sat planning his final *cavale*, his last escape."

You may have noticed that a few French words are blended into the dialogue. It is not necessary to write in dialect. Overuse of *"eet ees zee* way," and *"zat* was *zee* life," is distracting and begins to sound foolish. Anyway, now that we have Dreyfus off the island it's time to get back to Papillon. The *narrative* continues to illustrate the brutality of solitary confinement.

> Papillon survived five years in this solitary hell. His only guests were enormous eight-inch centipedes wider than "two fat fingers," with a sting that could leave a terrible burn. He learned to allow them to walk peacefully across his naked body.

Papillon described his feelings when he first stepped into his solitary cell on Saint Joseph: "I looked around my cell. It was hard to believe that a country like mine, France, the cradle of liberty for the entire world, the land that gave birth to the Rights of Man, could maintain, even in French Guiana, on a tiny island lost in the Atlantic, an installation as barbarously repressive as the Reclusion at Saint Joseph. Imagine 150 cells, back to back, their four-foot-thick walls pierced only by a small iron door. . . ." Papillon's cell featured a wooden bed, a wooden pillow, a pail for waste and a "ceiling made of iron bars as thick as streetcar tracks."

Note the *mixture of quotes, narrative and edited quotes*. Variety keep the reader turning pages. It's now time to get back to *character* and *dialogue*.

"Would you like to see the cemetery on Royale?" The Frenchman asked, interrupting my thoughts.

"Cemetery?" I questioned. "Weren't all the prisoners fed—buried at sea?"

He winked his open eye. "*Bagnards* were not the only ones to die on the islands." He turned and started up the pathway to the top of the island. I followed, climbing past the crumbling walls and the rusting bars of the former cells, past the empty shell of the warden's home, stepping over the encroaching undergrowth. Finally, we stopped at a small cemetery, a jumble of broken headstones blackened with tropical rot. The Frenchman removed his beret and said, "The children."

I looked closely at the few remaining inscriptions. Children. They were the graves of the children born on the islands to the wives of guards.

When I wandered around the island on my own, I stumbled across the tiny cemetery with twenty or so small graves with headstones. Many of marble plaques on the stones had been chipped off by tourists—or, perhaps, I mused, ghosts. Enough date-of-birth and date-of-death inscriptions remained to determine that the graves were of children. It was saddening to think that these children had lived their short lives in such a terrible place. I had the Frenchman mirror that emotion.

> The Frenchman looked sadly at me as he held his beret knotted in his hands. "They are now the quiet ghosts."
> I turned away and continued to the top of the hill. From there, the sea breeze blowing in my face, I could look at Saint Joseph and Devil's islands, two green tropical oases on a sea of blue. There was no sound other than the rustle of the breeze through the palm trees.
> And that sound was like a whisper of anguish.

The End

There you have it, a mix of ingredients to hold the reader's interest in a story that runs over 2,500 words. To achieve this mixture of techniques in your own writing, it is necessary to outline your article, choosing the different elements that best fit each part. To understand how this was done in the Devil's Island piece, here is an analysis of how the article was organized in outline form.

"Devil's Island" Outline

1. Hook: Frenchman talking about ghosts.
   (*Character, action, dialogue*)
2. Background and historical information:
   - Location of islands.
   - Who first arrived on the islands?
   - When did the French establish the penal colony, and when did it close?

- How do visitors get there?
  (*Narrative, anecdote*)
3. Frenchman explains "life was cheap" on the island. Prisoners buried at sea; fed to sharks.
  (*Character, action and dialogue*)
4. Show brutality of burial by using example from the book *Papillon*.
  (*Quotes, imagery*)
5. Begin walk around Royale with Frenchman. Reintroduce the *ghosts* concept.
  (*Narrative, character, dialogue*)
6. First sight of Devil's Island. Description.
  (*Narrative, imagery*)
7. Show what a prisoner's life was like on Devil's Island. Story of Captain Dreyfus. Quote from his diary.
  (*Narrative, quotes*)
8. Papillon's escape from Devil's Island. His time spent in solitary confinement on Saint Joseph Island.
  (*Quotes, anecdote, narrative*)
9. The children's cemetery on Royale. "The quiet ghosts."
  (*Narrative, character, dialogue*)
10. The end: The ghosts. "A sound like the whisper of anguish."
  (*Narrative*)

Rewriting Your Manuscript

"Writing is rewriting," the old cliché goes. Here's how "Devil's Island" was written—and rewritten. After completing the outline, the first draft was written from beginning to end. I did not worry about making revisions until the writing was complete. Here is how the rough *first draft* of the manuscript began:

If the very name sends a shiver through you, it's not surprising. Devil's Island was once part of France's most notorious prison settlement, to which generations of thieves, murderers and traitors were deported. No amount of sunlit sea or tropical palms can quite dispel the ghosts.

"The ghosts, they are here," the old man said, looking at the palm fronds swaying lightly in the breeze. "They brush against the trees in anguish."

Not very good, but I was just warming up. Once I wrote "brush against the trees in anguish," I knew the creative process had begun. From that rough beginning the *second draft* was written which read like this:

"Devil's Island: The Green Hell"
"The ghosts of the *bagnards*, the prisoners . . . they brush against the tree in anguish," the old Frenchman whispered in a deep accent as he listened to the air sighing through the palm trees.

"It's only the breeze from the ocean," I shrugged, not quite sure as I listened intently to the whispering sounds against the palm fronds.

The old Frenchman pouted with his lower lip, then shook his head slowly. "No, Monsieur . . . today the heat is heavy with them. In the air you can feel the weight of generations of *bagnards*. They are still here, imprisoned in their green hell."

From this, I wrote the *third* (and final) draft. Here is a paragraph-by-paragraph revision of the same lead:

Second Draft:

"The ghosts of the *bagnards*, the prisoners . . . they brush against the trees in anguish," the old Frenchman whispered in a deep accent as he listened to the air sighing through the palm trees.

Final Draft:

"*Oui monsieur,* the sound . . . it is the ghosts of the prisoners, the *bagnards* . . . They brush against the trees in anguish." The old Frenchman whispered the last word, "anguish," as he listened to the sighing of the palm trees.

Second Draft:

"It's only the breeze from the ocean," I shrugged, not quite sure as I listened intently to the whispering sounds against the palm fronds.

Final Draft:

"It is only the breeze from the ocean," I shrugged, not quite sure. There was a disturbing rustle of palm fronds.

Second Draft:

The old Frenchman pouted with his lower lip, then shook his head slowly. "No, Monsieur . . . today the heat is heavy with them. In the air you can feel the weight of generations of *bagnards.* They are still here, imprisoned in their green hell."

Final Draft:

The Frenchman pouted, shook his head slowly, then with heavy accent added, "No, *monsieur,* today the heat is heavy with them. In the air you can feel the weight of generations of *bagnards.* They are still here, imprisoned in the green hell of *l'Î'le du Diable*—imprisoned on Devil's Island."

How to Rewrite Your Article

Reread and rewrite until you are *reasonably* satisfied. Like Ernest Hemingway, who rewrote *A Farewell to Arms* thirty-seven times, you may never be *completely* satisfied. But there will come a time when continual rewriting will be counterproductive. Most writers settle on reworking a piece three to four times. The first draft is only an approximation. In the second and third drafts, you correct, delete and add. Finally, there is one last ruthless editing to prune extraneous words.

If you use a word processor, revising and rewriting can be relatively painless, although the process varies from writer to writer. If nothing else, it's simpler than retyping the manuscript three or four times. On a computer, I find that I rewrite and correct as I go, going back through a paragraph or a page and revising it (as I am doing now). The computer printout from that day's work is second-draft material. I then edit each page of printout with my handy ballpoint pen, making the final draft revisions on the word processor the next day.

WHAT SHOULD YOU LOOK FOR WHILE REWRITING?

- Check the lead. Those first 250 words are where your article lives or dies. Do you have a better way to begin the piece? Perhaps the best lead is on page three, or page four . . .
- Insure that you have arranged the points you want to cover in a logical order. Rearrange paragraphs so there are smooth transitions from idea to idea.
- Delete anything that departs from the slant of the article. A writer in my class wrote a piece on Naples, Italy, that included a side trip to Pompeii. I suggested that the writer cut the section on Pompeii as it was not the focus of the piece. The writer said she was reluctant to do so as she liked the way it was written. "Cut it," I encouraged her. She sold the article to a travel magazine and later told me that when she

submitted it, she left the Pompeii story in. "The editor cut it," she added.

- Keep paragraphs short. Too many novice writers, afraid to paragraph, ramble on for pages without a break. Forget what your English teacher said about the ideal paragraph containing *one idea* with the *topic* sentence at the beginning. We are talking about creative writing, not English Composition 101. How short should a paragraph be? A two-, three-, four-sentence paragraph is fine. Solid chunks of type can turn off even your most interested reader.

- Keep sentences short. For easy reading, sentences should vary in length. The average should be relatively short— between 10 and 25 words. Nothing is wrong with a four-word sentence. Or even a one-word sentence. (Right?) Careful, though, don't let your sentences get choppy. Variety . . . that's what makes writing readable.

- Choose the simple over the complex. You need both simple and complex forms to express ideas clearly. But remember, you're writing to *ex*press, not *im*press. If a shorter word, or a simpler word, can do the job, use it. Unless you are writing a treatise, write, "Try to find out," rather than "Endeavor to ascertain."

- Abstract words or phrasing dull your writing. Words like transubstantiation, circumspectly and juxtaposition are better off in the classroom. Just try to get through a 2,000-word article that begins: "Circumstances wherein considerable economies can be achieved . . ."

- Avoid unnecessary words. Nothing weakens writing more than using extra words. Be critical. Prune. Eliminate qualifying words such as *seems* and *perhaps*. Go through the text and see how many times you can cross out the word *that*.

- Limit the use of adjectives. If you have written "the dilapidated rustic brown crooked old barn," eliminate all the adjectives but one. As Voltaire said, "The adjective is the enemy of the noun."

- Use adverbs—those word modifiers that usually end in -ly—sparingly. Do you really need to write: "he said, angrily"? The preceding dialogue should *show* the character's anger.
- Use contractions whenever possible. "It's" and "I'm" are generally better than "It is" or "I am."
- Avoid roundabout phrases, such as *point of view*.
- Cut transitional words and phrases like *however, nevertheless* and *needless to say*.
- Use the active voice. The active voice sounds stronger than the passive. Stick with "I remember Mamma" rather than "Mamma will always be remembered by me." Use active verbs: "They opened the gate," rather than, "The gate was opened."
- **Cut** *all* clichés.

SHOULD YOU LEAVE TIME BETWEEN COMPOSITION AND REVISION?

Yes. Tuck your manuscript away in a drawer for a week, two weeks. Then you can approach it objectively and see where it went wrong or where it works as you wanted.

SHOULD YOU SHOW YOUR WORK TO OTHER READERS?

Yes—if the other readers are writers. It really isn't going to do much good to show your writing to your mother, cousin or boyfriend. You will either get a sweet, "Why, it's wonderful, darling," or a "What d'ya mean, you're a writer?" reply. You need someone who understands the writing process and can be objective about what you have written—a writer or an editor.

SHOULD YOU READ YOUR WRITING ALOUD?

Yes, read it aloud. It should flow easily and the sound of the finished product should communicate your ideas clearly. I always let writing students read their work in class. More often than not they are shocked by what they *hear*. A solid rewrite follows the reading.

Most writers feel that revision is at least as important as composition and spend more time with the rewriting process than they do with the original version. Oscar Wilde once said, "All morning I worked on the proof of one of my poems, and I took out a comma; in the afternoon I put it back in."

Yes, "Writing is rewriting."

How to Write "The End"

Thus far we have discussed how to write the beginning, the middle of the article and how to rewrite what you have written. But it's not finished. Not yet. Let's take a look at how to close out the piece.

How do you end an article? The last thing you ever want to write is, "In summary . . ." Save that for university term papers; it has no place in creative nonfiction. Yet you do need to end the article without letting the words dribble off the page as if you had nothing more to say. Here are two methods that work:

1. *Go back to the beginning.* Look at your lead. What did you say that could wrap up the story in a satisfying way? In the Devil's Island piece, I chose to go back and pick up the words, "and that sound was like a whisper of anguish." It repeated the mystery of the "ghosts."

2. *Search your material to see if you have an anecdote or quote that fits perfectly at the end.* This should be something that makes the reader think one last time about what you have said. When the reader comes to the words "The End" he

should feel a sense of satisfaction, and say to himself, "Now, I liked that. *That's* an interesting article." For instance, let's end this chapter with a quote: There is nothing to writing a 2,500-word article. All you have to do—as sportswriter Red Smith said—"is sit down at a typewriter and open a vein."

CHAPTER 7

Fiction Techniques in Nonfiction Writing

I always begin with a character, or characters, and then try to think up as much action as possible.

—John Irving

et's confront this *fiction* hangup face-to-face. Too many beginning writers look down their noses at nonfiction writing, saying it's not as *creative* as fiction. Nonfiction is supposed to be true, not entertaining, they say. The real writers are short story writers and novelists.

Rubbish! Writing is writing.

Author John Updike agrees. "If one sets up to be a writer," he says, "one should be able to write anything from a sonnet to a sermon, or at least be willing to try."

I once asked a well-known novelist what it took to have a

bestselling book. Without hesitation, he replied, "It must be a page-turner."

"How about nonfiction?" I questioned. "Do you apply the rule there also?"

"Why not? All the writer has to do is adapt the essential elements of fiction to produce readable, exciting nonfiction."

And that's the clue: *adapt the essential elements of fiction*. Let's take a look at how we can take fiction techniques and apply them to nonfiction.

In chapters five and six we had our first look at using fiction techniques when we discussed creating a scene and the use of character, action, dialogue, surprise, suspense, atmosphere and imagery. Now we need to provide a framework in which to use those essential fictional elements. That framework consists of: structure, story and plot.

Structure

The graph in the previous chapter illustrated the way a nonfiction article is structured. The graph on page 112 charts a fiction short story of 2,500 words (or a novel of 250,000 words):

Note that after the first major peak of 10 (the hook), the interest level falls off, as it did in the nonfiction graph. The variety of elements used to regain the reader's interest in nonfiction—character, action, dialogue, surprise, suspense, imagery—are also at the core of good fiction writing, but in fiction that interest level is intensified by *rising action*. The reader's interest should reach its peak as the story comes to the climax.

Story

The three pigs meet a hungry wolf and run off to their houses to hide.

That's the *story* behind "The Three Little Pigs."

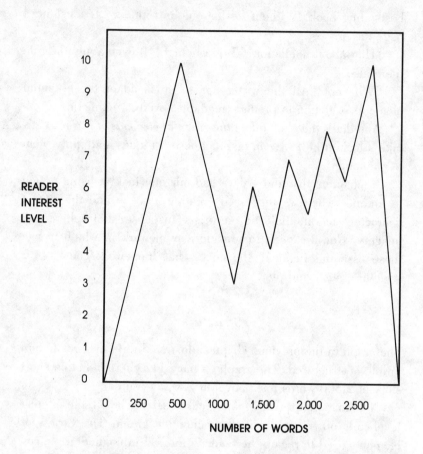

A story is charged with the implication that *something is going to happen* and that the story will come to a satisfactory conclusion.

You may notice that the above story does not tell what happened to the pigs. (That is the purpose of the *plot*, which will be discussed in a moment.)

Here's the lead from the first page of *Who Loves Brian? A Brother's Inside Story of the Beach Boys*, a book I ghost-wrote. These first 260 words set up the story:

What was left of the smog-filtered Los Angeles sunlight bore through the room's windows in slanted, yellow shafts.

I would have preferred being out in the smog, breathing deep, to what I was now facing. The sign hanging on the podium said, "The Greater Los Angeles Press Club." I took a deep breath, grasped my statement tightly in both hands and stepped to the microphone.

See how the *story* unfolds? The scene has been set. Although we don't yet know what's going on, we are hooked by the narrator's fear of what he is about to do. The story continues:

Video cameras flashed on, adding to the 100-degree temperature. The blue-white haze nearly obscured the row of television cameras and a dozen seated reporters. What if they turn against me? I thought. Am I in over my head? Is this the right thing to do?
Why is this room so damn hot?
The reporters, mostly women, were dressed casually in light summer clothes. I wore a gray suit and tie. My shirt stuck to my body and I could feel a bead of sweat trickling down my chest. *I'm going to smell like the inside of a gym bag.*
"Hello. Thank you for coming," I said, reminding myself to stand straight. If I bend my six-foot-eight-inch frame over the microphone I'll look like a question mark. I had spoken in front of larger audiences when I played professional basketball with the Los Angeles Lakers fifteen years earlier. But that was different. That had been for laughs, for some "inside" locker room stories. These reporters weren't here for entertainment—they were after a story.

Note how the character of the narrator is set up through his own inner thoughts. Expository material such as his height and basketball career is presented through the same method. There are several ways to show inner thoughts in a manuscript:
"What if they turn against me?" I thought.

What if they turn against me? I thought.
What if they turn against me? I thought.

Putting the thoughts in quotation marks is the least often used as it can be confused with dialogue. By underlining (italics), the thoughts are emphasized. Note how the last two methods are used in the above paragraphs. In this story, the reader can also *see, hear, smell* and *feel* the heat and the tension in the press room through the senses of the narrator. Let's finish setting the story:

> "This morning in Santa Monica Superior Court," I read, relieved to see the statement didn't shake in my hand, "I filed a petition to establish a conservatorship for Brian Wilson, my cousin, and founder of the Beach Boys . . ."
> That did it. There was a flurry of notetaking. Shutters clicked and motor drives buzzed.

That's it. The story—a man files a conservatorship to gain custody of his famous cousin—has been set up. The *plot* will now carry the story to its conclusion.

Plot

Plotting also plays an essential role in fiction. The plot is nothing more than a series of events (or scenes) that lead to a conclusion. Fiction writers refer to the plot as the *spine*. In its simplest form, the basic plot skeleton in a work of fiction is composed of four elements:

1. A *protagonist* (hero or heroine) who the reader can root for.
2. A *goal* for the protagonist to shoot for.
3. *Obstacles* placed in the path of the protagonist to keep him or her from achieving that goal. (An *antagonist* can also be introduced.)
4. The *climax*—the protagonist's achievement of the goal.

A well-known example of a story plotted in this manner is *Rocky*. The story of *Rocky* is simple: What if the *protagonist*, a pug fighter named Rocky Balboa (Sylvester Stallone), gets to fight for the heavyweight boxing championship? The plot "skeleton" begins when Rocky is offered the chance to fight the champion. In order to achieve this *goal*, Rocky must overcome certain *obstacles*. He is out of shape; he has a reluctant trainer/manager; his new girlfriend doesn't want him to fight. This struggle culminates in the emotional "Gotta fly now" scene where a rejuvenated Rocky charges up the steps, arms raised in triumph. With the audience rooting for him, the *climax* comes when Rocky fights the good fight, doesn't win, but achieves his goal to "go all the way."

Can the same structure used in *Rocky* be applied to a work of nonfiction? It would certainly work in a first-person personal experience story or a real-life-adventure drama. Could the technique work with a how-to article on building a tile patio? It would be less dramatic, to be sure, but why not create a couple of characters who build the sidewalk and discuss, in dialogue, its progress? (This technique is often used in televison home-improvement shows.) Mistakes (obstacles) could be made during the construction to show the reader what *not* to do. The successful completion of the patio (the goal) would end the article.

Most plotted stories are built around some kind of *conflict* in which the outcome is in doubt. Is Rocky still standing at the end of the fight? Do all three pigs evade the hungry wolf? The reader doesn't know the answer until the climax is reached.

AN EXERCISE IN THE USE OF FICTION TECHNIQUES

Let's take a look at the opening scene from Barnaby Conrad's nonfiction book, *Time Is All We Have*, a true story about the author's struggle with alcoholism and his treatment at the Betty Ford Center. As in a novel, the opening scene:

1. Sets up the story
2. Sets up the conflict

3. Sets the scene
4. Begins the action
5. Establishes a problem (and a goal to be achieved)
6. Creates suspense or mystery
7. Involves the reader in the action or emotion
8. Describes character traits
9. Uses imagery
10. Uses dialogue

See if you can pick out these ten elements in the first 100 words of *Time Is All We Have:*

I was lost. "Where's the clinic for drugs and alcohol?" I asked.

"The Center?" the policeman said.

That particular morning I wasn't afraid to pull up alongside the Palm Springs policeman's car; I had had a few, but I wasn't drunk, not according to their little Richter scale anyway. Just hung over and shaky from the day before—the days, weeks, months and years before.

"Hell, mister, you're a ways from Betty Ford's—that's over in Mirage. See that road there—it'll take you directly to it."

"Good name," I said. "Mirage."

He didn't seem to hear me.

It had taken me a long time to find the right road. Fear, more than hope, had brought me here.

Let's break this down and show the different fiction techniques Conrad uses in this opening scene:

1. *The story.* The first paragraph initiates the story line: the author, an alcoholic, is on his way to the Betty Ford Center for substance-abuse treatment.

2. *The conflict.* The author's conflict is with himself. Can he

conquer alcoholism? Conflict comes from three general sources: Man versus man; Man versus self; Man versus environment. In Conrad's story the conflict is man versus self.

3. *The scene*. This is like the stage setting for a play. In this case the opening scene takes place on a street corner, but the scene of the story will take place in the rehabilitation center.

4. *The action*. We're off and running fast—to the Betty Ford Center.

5. *The problem*. The line, "I was lost. 'Where's the clinic for drugs and alcohol?' " establishes the underlying problem that must be overcome: alcoholism.

6. *Suspense or mystery*. The story begins on a mysterious note: How did the author reach this point? "Fear, more than hope, had brought me here," Conrad states. What is he afraid of?

7. *Action and emotion*. The reader immediately gets involved in the action and emotion of the scene. Something is going to happen. Will the author succeed in his rehabilitation? Will he even find the place?

8. *Character*. The protagonist is established as the narrator. The use of inner dialogue—"I wasn't drunk, not according to their little Richter scale"—begins to define his character traits.

9. *Imagery*. The street corner anecdote is a complete scene, with a beginning, middle and end. Although the imagery is only implied, we can "see" the author leaning out of a window talking to the police officer.

10. *Dialogue*. The use of dialogue enables the author to open the scene in the middle of the action.

We have already discussed story, structure and plot, as well as character, action and imagery in previous chapters, but let's take a closer look at dialogue, one of the most important fiction techniques.

Dialogue

In 1989 Ten Speed Press published a nonfiction book whose entire story was told in dialogue. The book, *Publisher's Lunch*, by Ernest Callenbach, contained advice to writers on subjects such as advances, agents, delays in publishing, and book-signing parties. All the information was revealed in dialogue between a fictitious author and editor during six successive restaurant lunches.

While most new writers have a good ear for dialogue, they have difficulty with the simple mechanics of writing it. Too much of the time dialogue reads like this:

> "Good morning, Susan," she said.
> "Hi, Jane," she answered.
> "Want a cup of coffee?" Jane said.
> "Okay," Susan said.
> "Black?" Jane asked.
> "A little cream," she said.

Sounds dull, doesn't it? Actually, it's not even dialogue. It's conversation. In dialogue *something has to happen*. If Jane plans to dump a vial of arsenic in Susan's coffee, and the reader knows it, then we can call it dialogue.

The biggest problem with the above example is that the reader can't "see" the scene. Are we in a kitchen? We could be in a restaurant, in a living room, or on a patio.

Have characters occasionally *do* something during the dialogue to create visual images. Such as:

> "I don't care about your lousy birthday party!" he yelled, snuffing out his cigarette in the yolk of her poached egg.

Here's a rewrite of the Jane and Susan scene, using action to create imagery in dialogue. A bit of suspense has also been added:

"Good morning, Susan." Jane turned from the sink and dried her hands on her apron as her friend sagged into a chair at the kitchen table.

"Hi . . ."

Jane lifted the coffee pot off the gas burner and looked at her friend closely. "Want a cup of coffee?"

"Okay." She absently twisted the engagement ring around her finger.

"Black?"

"A little cream." Susan squeezed her eyes shut, trying to hold back the tears.

See how quotation marks break up the page, just as in fiction? It makes the page look less blocky and easier to read. How many times have you turned the page of a book, seen a solid mass of black type and thought, *I have to read through all this?* And how many times have you come across two pages of dialogue with lots of white space and thought how easy it was going to be to read those pages? As a bonus, dialogue gives your story "eye appeal."

EXERCISE IN THE USE OF DIALOGUE #1

Here is a sample that could easily win the lousiest dialogue of the year award at any writers' conference. See if you can recognize the mistakes:

Sally is sitting in the living room eating a box of chocolates when Jim crashes through the front door.

"Sally!' he says, angrily.

"Jim!' she says. "Why are you here? You're supposed to be at work for another forty-seven minutes."

"Sally," he said, "can't you stop stuffing chocolates down your gullet? I can't stand it anymore. I've had all I can take. I've had it up to here. I'm finished. Through. It's over. Over!"

"Over?" she asks.

"Yeah, do you think I haven't heard about your affair with Sam Throckmeyer? About the hotel room you two have been meeting at on 1255 Maple Street next door to the Racquet Club and across the street from the Double Bar Restaurant for the last six and a half months and three days?"

"That's not true," she said.

"How long did you think you could hide behind sheep's clothing and pull the wool over my eyes? All those weeks you said you were visiting your Aunt Gertrude in Santa Monica! Well, Sally, I know your aunt's been dead and buried for six months in Forest Lawn Cemetery—lot 226."

"Jim, for the love of heaven . . ."

"Love," he said, "you call this love? I don't love you, I hate you, Sally. I can't stand the sight of you."

Jim yanks a gun out of his belt.

Sally says, "Jim, where did you buy that gun?"

"I'm going to put a bullet through your cheating heart, Sally. I'm going to shoot you. I'm going to kill you. Kill you dead. Yes, Sally—dead."

"Jim, please . . ."

"Goodbye, Sally."

"Jim . . ."

He fires the gun. She grasps her chest and drops in a heap on the couch.

What makes this dialogue so trite?

First, did you notice all the "he saids" and "she saids"? Phrases indicating who is speaking are fine as long as they don't become intrusive. Readers do not realize they are reading "he said" directions if they are used sparingly, just enough to keep the reader aware of which character is speaking. On the other hand, be careful not to lose your reader. Make sure you do use the directions when needed. All of us have read dialogue in which we lost track of who was speaking and had to backtrack several lines to figure it out.

2. Note that the tense changes several times from "he said" to "he says." Once you have established the present or past tense, stick with it.

·3. "Sally"? "Jim"? Didn't you get weary of hearing those names repeated? In dialogue, use the name of the other character judiciously, not every line. Think about it—how often do you repeat someone's name in conversation?

4. There is too much expository material. Do we need to know that Sally has been meeting Sam Throckmeyer at 1255 Maple Street next door to the Racquet Club and across the street from the Double Bar Restaurant for the last six and a half months and three days? Or that Aunt Gertrude has been dead and buried for the last six months in Forest Lawn Cemetery—lot 226?

5. There is too much repetition. "I'm through. Finished. It's over," and, "I'm going to shoot you. I'm going to kill you. Kill you dead." It's enough to drive any reader to the aspirin bottle.

6. "Where did you buy that gun?" Who cares where he bought the gun? This isn't an argument over shopping. He's going to shoot her.

7. How about the phrases, "I've had it up to here," "dead and buried," "pull the wool over my eyes," and "your cheating heart"? All are clichés and should be eliminated. Yes, a person *can* speak in clichés, but only if doing so defines his or her character. Using clichés is the sign of a lazy writer. How about the following, for example?

Clichés are a dead giveaway that a writer is bone idle. An eager-beaver writer should be able to rack her brain and run circles around run-of-the-mill writers. Once she gets her feet wet, the writer will be able to take off like a ball of fire.

EXERCISE IN THE USE OF DIALOGUE #2

Rewrite the Sally and Jim scene using the elements of good dialogue. Build to the climax. Make it dramatic, not trite.

Analyzing a Nonfiction Personal Experience Story

Let's analyze a simple nonfiction personal experience piece to see how the use of fiction techniques make the story come alive.

Of Barrels and Butterflies
by Kim Millner

> I sit restlessly in the saddle, then lean forward in antici-
> pation as I hear the announcement of the rodeo's next event:
> "Ladies and Gentlemen, it's time for barrel racing!"

This sets the scene: we are at a rodeo and watching a barrel-racing event. The narrator will obviously be participating in the race. Note that the story is told in the *first person* and the *present tense*.

> As the first rider—a 17-year-old girl—dashes across the
> starting line, my stomach begins to fill with the familiar
> butterflies and my palms become sweaty. But I shout en-
> couragement to her. I am fixed on the movement of the
> horse and rider as they whirl around the cloverleaf pattern
> in which the three barrels are placed.

Now we know the age of the participants in the race—teenagers—and a little bit about the event itself.

> Then I begin to visualize myself and my horse in the place
> of the rider in the outdoor arena. We are galloping toward
> the finish line. I lean forward on my horse's neck and can
> hear the pounding of her hoofs hitting the ground, smell
> the sweat from her flanks. We cross the finish line; my
> heart is racing . . .
>   "Seventeen point three seconds!" the announcer booms.
>   The voice shakes me back to reality: 17.3 seconds! A
> fast time. I'll never beat that time. Never!

At this point the story is set. We have a barrel racer—the *pro-tagonist*—whose *goal* is to win the race. To do that, the racer will have to overcome certain *obstacles:* a fast time to beat, her own fears, and the technical difficulties of the race itself. Now that the action has started, the narrative shifts to the *past tense*, to show the events that led up to the race.

> The evening before the rodeo, I had cleaned and polished my bulky Western saddle until my fingers ached; I shined my boots until I could see my reflection in the toes. Then I pressed my silver-studded shirt and the Levi's which are still stiff from newness.

There is no reason why the story couldn't begin with the line, "The evening before the rodeo. . . ." No reason except that it's dull in comparison to the action lead. Start your story when the action begins, then flash back to the events that led up to that action.

> I awoke at dawn, collected my clothes, grabbed an extra bunch of carrots and headed for the stables. That is where I found my dapple-gray friend, Alegria, in her stall munching on her last bit of alfalfa. I put on her halter and led her outside to the cleaning block. This was where she'd be tethered for the next several hours while I fussed and puttered around her, preparing for the barrel-racing event.
>   I bathed her like a giant puppy, using the same shampoo I used to wash my own hair earlier in the morning. I combed her gray and white tail until it shone like strands of silver tinsel. Then I buffed her hooves with black polish befitting a parade steed.

This is good use of *imagery*, with such phrases as "bathed her like a giant puppy," and "shone like strands of silver tinsel."

> Finally, mussed and dirty, but with Alegria glowing, I returned her to her stall and headed for the stable's bath-

room, which had been transformed into a dressing room crowded with teenage cowgirls, all primping to get ready. It was less than an hour to the barrel racing event, but the time passed quickly.

"Eighteen seconds flat!" the rodeo announcer says loudly over the speaker.

We have now transitioned back to the barrel-racing event by using the present tense. Note how the phrase "but the time passed quickly" smoothly segues into the action. From this point on the reader wonders who will win the race.

Alegria's ears twitch and she rubs her nose against the arena fence. I lean forward, the saddle creaking under me, and coo a few soothing words in her ear, wondering if she has butterflies in her stomach. We'll be called into the arena soon.

The next rider receives a five-second penalty for knocking down one of the three barrels. The audience groans in sympathy.

The following rider is my friend, Jodi, and I edge Alegria closer to the fence to watch her ride and cheer her on. She returns beaming, having completed a fantastic ride; "Seventeen point five!" cries the voice on the loudspeaker.

The first rider's time of 17.3 seconds is still the time to beat.

"Next we have rider number five, Kim Millner, riding Alegria."

The stage is set—the fight for the championship is about to begin. Will this rider win?

I give Alegria a nudge in the ribs with my heels and move into the ring. Entering the gate, she begins to prance about restlessly. She has been in this ring before and knows what is required. I allow her to take a moment to eye the barrels and ready herself. Then I let the reins out and give her a jab with my heels.

We're off at a gallop!

As in *Rocky*, the bell has just sounded for the fight to begin.

The first barrel is the trickiest for us; we have to make a right turn around it, not the turn Alegria favors. I tighten the reins and pull her around the barrel, careful to keep her turn tight.

On to the second barrel where we will make a left turn, creating a figure eight. We start the turn too close and my knee brushes the barrel. As we head for the center and the final turn, I hear the crowd moan as the barrel totters in place.

Did I knock it over?

Suspense! Did the barrel fall? A five-second penalty would cause the rider to lose the race. Obstacles have been put in the path of the rider to make it more difficult to reach her goal. Also note that the rules of the barrel race are *shown* with action during the actual event, rather than with expository paragraphs that *tell* how the race is conducted.

No time to look; we gallop to the last barrel. We take it a little wide, but can make up for the lost time on the home stretch. I hear Alegria's hooves thundering under me and feel the wind in my face as she stretches out at her fastest stride.

We cross the finish line and I tug at the reins, bringing Alegria to a walk. I quickly turn in the saddle and catch a glimpse of the second barrel. No, it didn't fall.

The gate opens and we walk out of the arena. I lean forward and give Alegria a loving pat on the neck. Then the announcement: "Kim's time, seventeen point four seconds!"

We've won second place!

I am extremely proud as we enter the ring to collect our ribbon. The judge hooks the vibrant-red ribbon onto Alegria's bridle and we canter around the arena to the music of the audience's applause.

I smile.

The butterflies are gone.

The End

Okay, so the rider didn't win. (But then, neither did *Rocky* in the first fight.) This piece was written by an unpublished writer, my daughter, Kim Millner, in a college creative writing class. I thought it was good enough for publication, and, after very minor editing, sent it to *Horse and Horseman* magazine, where it was published.

Outline for "Of Barrels and Butterflies"

The outline for the story was done in five simple steps:

1. Lead: a rodeo arena, with a protagonist waiting for a barrel-racing event to begin.
   (*Set the scene* with *character, action, dialogue*)
2. Announce the time the heroine has to beat in order to win the race.
   (A *protagonist* with a *goal* and *obstacles* to overcome.)
3. Provide background information before the race.
   (*Exposition* and *imagery*)
4. Transition to the arena. The race begins.
   (*Action, suspense*)
5. The race ends. The protagonist takes second place.
   (*Character, action*)

There you have it: a nonfiction personal experience story in which fictional techniques have been applied to bring life to a potentially prosaic plot line. *Your* personal experience story can fit into the same structure. Try it.

As author John Gardner said, "Through the study of technique—not canoeing or logging or slinging hash—one learns the best, most efficient way of making characters come alive, learns the difference between emotion and sentimentality, learns to discern, in the planning stages, the difference between the better dramatic action and the worse. It is this kind of knowledge . . . that leads to mastery."

The Q's and A's of Interviewing

Judge a man, not by his answers, but by his questions.

—Voltaire

"Madam, Adam."

"Eve."

And so began the world's first interview. The ensuing question and answer session must have been fascinating. Unfortunately, there wasn't a third party, a writer with a tape recorder on the scene to record it.

What if Howard Cosell had been there to interview David and Goliath before their big fight? What if Barbara Walters had been on hand to chat with Cleopatra and Mark Antony? What if Mike Wallace had been able to confront Genghis Khan? What if *any* of today's interviewers had been there to question Shakespeare on the opening night of *Hamlet?*

Would those people have agreed to an interview? Of course. From the beginning of time people have delighted in talking about themselves. Answering questions gives an individual an air of importance and boosts his or her ego. As journalist/interviewer A. J. Liebling said, "We are an articulate people, pleased by attention, covetous of being singled out." Fortunately for the writer, people love to talk about themselves, their work, and their personal expertise.

Quotations Lend Credibility

A writer can't know everything. You may want to write an article on divorce settlements. Who do you interview? A divorce attorney. Let's say you are writing a story on Columbus' perilous first journey across the Atlantic to the New World. Who do you interview? An historian with expertise in that era. Want to write a piece on Mom and Pop grocery stores? Who do you interview? Mom and Pop.

A student writer decided to write an article about ATMs, the automatic tellers that banks use to provide patrons with day-and-night cash and deposit facilities. Who did the writer interview? Her husband—an ATM repairman! From him she got great quotes—"Look, Sara, there *is* a man in that machine!"—and wrote the story.

Getting firsthand, expert quotes will beef up any nonfiction work and make it more saleable. Learning the interviewing process will enable the writer to add vitality, credibility and an authoritative voice to a manuscript.

Where do you find these experts? It's as simple as running your fingers through the Yellow Pages. Anyone, from magicians to marble cutters, from wine consultants to zoologists, can be found in the telephone book. You can also try the *Who's Who* series of books at your library.

Getting these "experts" to agree to a brief interview, especially a telephone interview, is easy. Professionals like to make statements, to show their expertise, to see their names in print. Just explain what you are doing—"I'm writing an article on emergency care centers, called 'The McDonald's of Medicine,' and I'd like to get your opinion of their place in the medical profession." You'll get answers.

For my article about television game-show contestants, "The TV Games People Play," for *The Saturday Evening Post*, I interviewed Mark Goodson, known as "TV's godfather of game shows." The quotes I got from him about the type of contestant he was looking for added richness and *credibility* to my story. "I can recognize a good contestant when he walks into the room," Goodson said. "He's got to have lively eyes. . . ."

Selecting a Subject for a Personality Profile

In *The Craft of Writing*, William Sloane said: "There are no uninteresting subjects, only uninteresting writers."

You don't have to interview Kathleen Turner or Harrison Ford to sell a magazine article. Interesting people to interview for a feature story—the personality profile—are everywhere. They may be that twenty-two-year-old woman down the street who opened a low-cal ice cream shop, or that man around the corner who collects beer bottles.

Interview the common person who has done something uncommon.

Check the features section of your local newspaper. Feature editors are constantly discovering interesting people to write about. You can inteview the same person for a magazine or another journal.

Here's the headline for a feature story that appeared in the Santa Barbara daily newspaper: GRAD DOESN'T KID: BOOKS SICKENING.

The story was about a graduate student with a unique problem: books put her to sleep—literally! Due to an allergic reaction to the chemicals in paper, she had to study her books in an enclosed glass box. What a great human interest story on how to overcome a handicap!

Making Contact

I suggest writing a letter to the person you want to interview, clearly stating what you are going to write about and why you would like to have that person's opinions. You can do a little buttering up—"I understand you are the premier authority in this area"—but don't make it sound like idol worship. If you are on assignment to write the story for a specific magazine, say so. Advise the interviewee that you will telephone to set up the interview.

Choosing the Interview Setting

Where should the interview take place? There are several possibilities, some good, some bad. With professional people, it may be advantageous to do the interview at their office or work area. You can see how they go about their job, what pressures they are under and how well they cope with business and career problems. Just realize interruptions are inevitable. An office is a busy place, with phones ringing, secretaries scurrying about, and so forth.

For a full-length personality interview, the individual's home is the best place. Interviewees are more comfortable in their own surroundings and you can observe them on their own turf.

The last resort is a restaurant. Lunches are a writer's best friend, but a busy restaurant is a lousy place to conduct a taped interview. A tape recorder with a condenser mike will pick up every sound within a twenty-foot circle.

Interviewing by Telephone

If you are unable to do the interview in person, a telephone interview will provide the answers you need. The telephone is an excellent and immediate way of gathering information, especially if you need answers to just a few questions. Besides, you won't have to travel 200 or 2,000 miles to talk to the subject. The big disadvantage is that you can't *see* your subject, and you miss out on body language, facial expressions and the opportunity to view the person's work space. Also, phone interviews start out rather cold. If you have never met the individual before, it is difficult to establish a rapport.

If you are tape-recording the phone conversation—and I highly suggest you do—the interviewee must be advised that he or she is being taped. Don't make a big project of it, simply say something like, "I'm terrible at taking notes, so I'll have to record our interview." As long as you don't hear "No," on the other end of the line, you can record the conversation. (You can purchase an attachment that connects your tape recorder to the telephone at an electronics specialty store like Radio Shack.)

Doing Advance Research

It doesn't matter if you're going to interview an expert for five minutes or a movie star for an hour, you must still prepare for the interview by researching the subject and delving into his or her area of expertise. If you are going to interview a doctor of medicine, an attorney, or a business person, talk to friends and associates who can brief you on the vocabulary and basics of that profession. Pick up a book at the library and use it as resource material so you can begin to understand your subject.

At the library, you may also find articles that have been written about the interviewee. Previously published material may provide quotes that you will want to refer to in your interview. Ask the subject for further comments in light of the present situation.

Remember, it is your responsibility to gather information and prepare questions before the interview begins. *Don't go into it cold.* If you do, you won't get the quotes you need for your article.

Preparing the Questions

Writers who conduct *Playboy* interviews do research in such depth that they come up with hundreds of questions. How many questions are necessary? For a short interview, for the purpose of getting the opinion of an expert on a specific subject, one or two pointed questions may suffice. Between ten and twenty questions will cover most full-length (hour-and-a-half) interviews. Even five questions can be enough, as one question will lead to another. The idea is to have five *good* questions.

Run your list of questions through this test to determine their value:

1. *Are the questions short, clear and concise?* The world's worst questions are asked at presidential press conferences. Journalists seem to pride themselves on asking confusing, three-part questions that obscure the focus in a jungle of jargon, fractured syntax and endless rephrasing.
2. *Will the questions produce quotable quotes?* You want to get great answers—fresh, vibrant quotes that are alive and breathe with the personality of the subject.
3. *Will the questions dig out feelings as well as facts?* If you are going to interview a prominent person who's been through the standard twenty-question routine, you had better come up with questions that dig deeper. Ask them how they *feel* about something, such as a heart-wrenching divorce.
4. *Do the questions cover the subject's past? The present? The future?* The old, "How did you get started in your profession?" and "What has been the most important thing in your life?" are great ways to begin—and end.
5. *Do the questions gloss over any controversy?* It's tough to ask penetrating, no-nonsense questions, but if the answers are necessary to your story, ask them.

6. *Eliminate all questions that can be answered with a simple "yes" or "no."* For example, don't ask: "Was Marlon Brando a difficult actor to work with?" Reword your question: "*Why* was Marlon Brando a difficult actor to work with?" Questions that begin with the words *what, why, when, where* or *how* are impossible to answer with a "yes" or a "no."

Using the Tape Recorder

There are only two reasons for not using a tape recorder during an interview:

1. You have the memory of an elephant.
2. You can write twelve words per second in longhand.

The tape recorder is one of the most valuable editorial tools in today's writing business. Trade in your pad and pencil for a light-weight, inexpensive, battery-powered cassette recorder. A tape recorder leaves you free to observe and listen. It also gets the quotes down accurately. One important note: Make sure you have fresh batteries in your recorder (and take spares) before leaving for the interview.

Starting the Interview

The interview session is only a few moments away. You're standing at the front door of the interviewee's home, tape recorder and notebook in hand. You check your watch. Yep, right on time— to the minute. Everything is perfect, except for the butterflies that are kicking up a bacchanalia in your stomach. You're nervous. That's okay. It's perfectly normal to be nervous when you're going to an interview—whether it's your first time out or your fiftieth.

Just remember, the subject you are going to interview is more frightened than you. Many people hold writers in great reverence, and are in awe of their creative art. They believe Edward Bulwer-

Lytton's quote that "the pen is mightier than the sword." Confronted by a writer armed with a pen, notebook and tape recorder, interviewees may be terrified of not being able to come up with articulate answers. The pressure is on them, not you. Even celebrities can be terrified of interviews. Comedian Steve Martin agonizes over interviews and admits: "I hope he doesn't ask me *that*."

People are also concerned with what you will say about them in the completed article. Will you write the piece honestly, without taking the subject's words out of context?

Ava Gardner once said, "People are always asking me why I don't give more interviews. The answer is simple: I'm tired of all the lies that have been written about me. The last time I trusted an interviewer, he crucified me."

Establishing a Rapport with the Interviewee

Going on an interview is really like going on a blind date. You are both trying to be liked, you both want to show the best possible side and win each other over. The subject wants to put forth the best image of himself. And this plays to your advantage. What the interviewee is going to show of himself in those first few minutes is very revealing.

You're now inside the front door. Look around, observe the furnishings, the decorations, photographs, style of decor, color of the walls—everything. You can learn a lot about a person from the way he or she decorates a home.

If the subject offers you a cup of coffee or a glass of soda, say yes. While he is away brewing or pouring, take the opportunity to study the surroundings. Make mental notes of everything in the room.

Look around for something that the individual takes great joy in, such as a hobby, perhaps a collection of toy soldiers or paperweights, match covers or first editions . . . anything. When the subject returns with the coffee, make a comment about his hobby or collection. Odds are it will trigger a relaxed discussion.

Studs Terkel has a technique of relating to the subject by discussing his own experiences. "I'll say things to lead the person on," he says, "something like, 'Oh yeah, that happened to me.' You see, if I bring some of my own stuff in, maybe that person will feel more akin to it."

Be careful with this technique. Terkel's idea may work with people who have never been interviewed before as a way to get them to start talking, but the last thing you want to do at an interview is spend the time hashing over your own life.

An interview is a process of gaining trust, then gaining information. You are in control of the interview, and it's your responsibility to establish a rapport with the individual. It's really not that tough a job. Just remember—the *subject* wants the interview to be successful too.

Three Interviewing Rules

1. *Show genuine interest.* There is more to the interview than smiles and warmth. An interview also involves honesty. If you demonstrate an air of integrity and consideration for the person you are interviewing, your reward will be a rewarding session.

2. *Try a little flattery.* You're not trying to apple-polish, but it's a good idea to keep the subject's ego satisfied.

   "I know you're considered one of the best architects . . . "

   "Your expertise with raising a family has been well noted. What advice would you give to a young married couple?"

   When you make your subject feel like an authority, you'll get strong, positive quotes instead of a stream of "I don't knows," and "That might be true."

3. *Don't interrupt!* Let the subject finish sentences and complete his thoughts. The subject must fill the space, and

he'll usually fill it with something he didn't think he'd say (or hoped he wouldn't say). Mike Wallace says, "The single most interesting thing you can do in an interview is to ask a good question and then let the answer hang there for two or three seconds as though you are expecting more. And, you know what? They get a little embarrassed and they give you more."

Settling In

Now it's time to start the questions. Make sure the seating arrangement is close enough for eye contact—and for the tape recorder.

When you are comfortably seated, *turn on the tape recorder*, and say, "This is a nice quiet place to use the tape recorder." By saying this, you are, in essence, asking and receiving permission to record the session. It would be very unusual if the person did not agree to a recorded interview. However, if the subject says something to the effect that he didn't realize he was going to be taped, then simply state that you tape all your interviews. You can assure the subject that no one else will have access to the tape.

It's time to open your notebook to your list of questions. You should have left some space on the notebook page so that you can take notes. You may want to write down how your subject sits, moves his hands, what he wears.

Now you're ready for the first question.

Popping the Questions

The first question. You ask the simplest, nicest, Kansas-schoolboy question you can think of. "Gee, you grew up in Wichita, Kansas. Why, that's only 125 miles from Kansas City, where I grew up." Now, maybe that sounds a little too homey, but in the beginning you're simply trying to get the conversation going. News journalist Red Barber liked to use trivial questions to begin an interview. "A human being likes to stick his toe into water that isn't cold," Barber once said. "I always start with a pleasantry."

The first questions should be low-key and *easy* to answer, yet be of special interest to the subject. Try the kind of questions that are actually conversation-openers:

"I read that your Chardonnay won a gold medal at the Monterey wine judging . . ."

"I see that your book, *Women Who Love Too Much*, has been on the bestseller list for eight months."

Make those first questions pertain to the subject's specialty. Bankers feel comfortable talking about assets, politicians, about their pet piece of legislation, actors, about their latest film, writers, about their newest book, and antique collectors, about their latest acquisitions.

Keep all questions short, clear and to the point. Don't force the subject to work to understand the question, make them work to *answer* it. Don't ask, "Do members of an avian species of identical plumage congregate?" when you mean, "Do birds of a feather flock together?"

Don't start with viciously penetrating questions such as, "Your last movie was criticized as being a violent piece of trash. What do you say about that?" The subject may answer with stunned silence. He won't think, "Wow! I sure wasn't prepared for that." More likely he'll be thinking, "What a jerk this person is!" There goes the rapport, and it may take half an hour to get back on track—if you ever do.

Asking Dumb Questions

Is there such a thing as a dumb question? Some interviewers feel the only real stupid question is the one that was never asked. "Tell me a little about what you have accomplished," *is* a dumb question. The interviewer had better *know* what the subject has done. If you have researched properly, you will already know a good percentage of the answers.

Sometimes questions will tumble out of an interviewer's mouth that have a different meaning than intended. Even Phil Donahue is not immune to the television blooper. "I once asked a psychiatrist if male impotence was on the rise," Donahue admits.

On the other hand, don't be afraid to ask for clarification on an answer. It's *not* dumb to say, "I don't understand." That's an honest response and the subject will feel good about filling you in on what he knows.

Future, Present and Past

Questions can be divided into three categories, the future, the present and the past.

THE FUTURE

This line of questioning gets to the "hot stuff" right away. Everyone is more interested in what's going to happen than what has happened.

Don't be too broad in scope: "What projects are you planning?"

Instead, be specific: "I understand you have been contracted to star in *The Blue World*. What kind of character do you play?"

This is better, as it shows that you already know what project the subject is going to be working on. You have done your homework.

THE PRESENT

Instead of "future" questions, you may want to start with "present" questions.

"What are you working on now?"

Or even better: "I understand that in your research you have discovered a new vaccine . . ."

THE PAST

Finally, you can delve into history.

"When were you born?"

Or better: "What year were you born?"

Or even better, "At what age did you get started in your profession?"

The "how did you get started" line of questioning allows the subject to relax, get used to the tape recorder (and forget it's there) and become accustomed to your questioning style. As the session continues and the interviewee warms up, slip in questions that are harder to field.

Asking the Right Question

Don't use your list of questions as a checklist. Don't methodically mark each one off. The interview may be a fairly structured situation, but if something new, unique or surprising crops up then, home in on it. Often, during the course of the interview, you will find precisely the right question that strikes the perfect note and unlocks a floodgate of information. It's the question that occurs to you because of something the subject said. That is why it is so important to listen and really care about what the person is saying. You'll come up with a question that you never would have thought of in advance, one that you didn't discover in your research.

You acquire information only when the subject is speaking, not when you are. So bring your questions directly to the point, and don't talk about yourself unless asked. The subject is there to talk about himself and quickly becomes bored with what you have to say.

Listen! Listen! Listen!

Few novice interviewers are good listeners. They concentrate so hard on the next question that they lose track of the conversation.

There's a story (which probably never happened) about an historian interviewing Alice Roosevelt Longworth, daughter of President Teddy Roosevelt. The interviewer had his head buried in his notes and was firing off one question after another. Noticing that the interviewer wasn't listening, Alice Roosevelt answered a question, then added, "And of course, on Wednesday afternoon we all had to leave the White House because my father brought in his mistress." The historian said, "Now, Mrs. Longworth, about the locks on the Panama Canal . . ."

He missed it! He didn't *listen*.

Now, there *is* a difference between listening and being mute. An interview is still a conversation between two people. The only difference is that one of the people, the interviewer, is orchestrating the course of the conversation. The skill of a great listener lies in knowing when to talk and when to shut up. If the interviewer is mesmerized by his own patter, the interview will end up a shambles.

Getting the Great Quote

Interviewees like to talk in generalities. They may pop off with some good quotes that will spice up the profile, but for the most part it will be pretty dull stuff. Few can match Cher when she commented on turning forty—"I'm not like Jane Fonda or any of those other women who say how fabulous they think it is to turn forty. I think it's a crock of shit." No one could mistake that for an android talking. Or Robert Mitchum's response when an interviewer asked him what he did for exercise. Mitchum shrugged and said, "I breathe in, I breathe out."

As good as these crackling sharp quotes are, they are hard to come by. Many times the interviewer has to pry them out of the interviewee. I once asked a rock musician, "What was the concert like?"

"Oh, it was great!" came the reply.

"Uh, tell me how it *felt* to be there. What did you *hear, see* and *feel?*"

"Oh, it was *really* great!"

I kept pressing with questions like: "Was there one concert you remember above all others?" and "Can you recall a special moment at a concert that made your heart leap with joy?" The answer finally came tumbling out, a forgotten memory that was awakened in the mind. It said a lot more than, "Oh, it was great!"

Quotes that contain imagery, ones the reader can "see," are the excellent responses. Such as this quote from actor Don Murray, who starred with Marilyn Monroe in *Bus Stop*. Here's how he responded when asked about his first meeting with the blond sex goddess:

> Marilyn had this aura . . . I was in her dressing room, and she was stretched out on this white couch. She had just come from the shower wrapped in a white terry-cloth robe. She had that marvelous platinum hair. No makeup, just a little baby oil on her face, that smooth lineless face . . . It was an impressive picture, totally breathtaking.

Studs Terkel, who considers himself a gold prospector when looking for powerful quotes, came across some real nuggets in preparing his book of personal interviews on World War II, *The Good War*. Terkel got the following quote from a marine who remembered a Japanese gunner who'd had the top of his head blown off in battle:

> He was just sitting upright in front of the machine gun . . . His eyes were wide open. It had rained all night and the rain had collected inside his skull. . . . I noticed a buddy of mine just flippin' chunks of coral into the skull about three feet away. Every time he'd get one in there, it'd

splash. It reminded me of a child throwing pebbles into a puddle.

Going for the Tough Stuff

The interview has been going along smoothly for an hour now. The interviewee is relaxed and having a good time. You feel it's time to pop the tough questions. But be careful; getting tough may mean getting put down.

Broadcast journalist Sander Vanocur learned his lesson when he interviewed Rita Hayworth:

VANOCUR: How is a sex goddess manufactured?

HAYWORTH: That's impossible to tell unless you have several hours.

VANOCUR: I have.

HAYWORTH: (testily): Well, I haven't.

Howard Cosell always had a knack for asking tough, penetrating questions—and getting away with it. He once asked the English boxer Brian London (who was scheduled to fight heavyweight champion Muhammad Ali) this question:

"Brian, they say you are a pug, a patsy, a dirty fighter, and that you have no class, that you're just in there for the ride and the fast payday and that you have no chance against Ali. Now what do you say to that?"

Another tough interviewer is Alex Haley. Before he wrote *Roots*, he was noted for his *Playboy* interviews with difficult personalities. Haley said he did it this way: "You soften them up while you prepare for the tough ones." To do this, Haley would take his subjects for a ride or for lunch and exchange stories with them. "Then," Haley says, "you can get them to the point where you can play them like a harp."

Being Observant

Throughout the interview observe your subject carefully. He or she will be doing most of the talking, so there will be time to watch. Look for unusual character traits in your subject's body language and dress. If he is wearing Gucci shoes and white sweat socks, that's a clue to his temperament and lifestyle.

Watch body language and hand gestures closely. How does the subject sit? Slumped? Straight-backed? Relaxed? Tense? Look at hand gestures. Do the fingers tap nervously? Does she brush her long hair away from her face with the palm of her hand? Does he pick at his nails? You may want to use some of these details when it comes time to write the article.

Look at the way the subject is dressed. How did he prepare for the interview? Actor Karl Malden padded to the front door in stocking feet. Bo Derek was bundled up in a padded nylon jacket, jeans and boots. Jonathan Winters had on Marine Corps camouflage fatigues. Jimmy Stewart was nattily attired in a blue blazer and tie.

Be perceptive. You must try to look deep inside a person. Try to put yourself in his place. Try to feel what he is feeling, think the way he's thinking. He will feel that empathy and begin to open up. When this happens, you can get to the truth and discover the real person.

Alfred Kinsey, the sexual behaviorist, was once asked how he could be positive that the intimate details a person was telling him were true. Kinsey replied, "I look them straight in the eye. I lean forward, stare them in the eye and rapidly ask one question after the other. If they falter, I can tell if they're lying."

Off-the-Record

If the subject says, "This is off-the-record," you must honor that by not using the quote. The strict definition of the term is that statements made off-the-record are not to be published. The writer can use them as background information only. If during the interview the subject goes on and on after saying "this is off-the-record," you should ask if what he is saying is *still* off-the-record.

The Quotable Quote

It's a good idea to come to an interview armed with a few pertinent quotations from other sources. Borrow something from Mark Twain or Will Rogers or the Bible. If interviewing a successful writer, you could ask, "Samuel Johnson said that no man but a blockhead ever wrote except for money. How do you feel about that?"

When I interviewed broadcast journalist Ralph Story, I quoted from author Gay Talese: " 'Most journalists are restless voyeurs who see warts on the world . . . gloom is their game, the spectacle their passion, normality their nemesis.' Do you feel that's true?" Story paused thoughtfully. "I think he's right—to a degree," he said. "You have to remember it's a reporter's job to find those warts, to prod and probe, to get in the way, to be curious, to be annoying, even to be vicious . . . We're really not persecuting; it's just our business to pry."

Prying is the business of the interviewer.

When to Stop the Interview

If you are doing your job as an interviewer by watching your subject closely, you will know when to quit. If he or she starts peeking at a watch, or yawning, or the eyes wander, or the pauses keep getting longer and longer, it's time to end the session.

The normal time for a full-length interview session is from an hour and a half to two hours. Anything longer than that and the subject will become too tired to respond effectively. *You* will also be burned out. An interview is hard work for both parties, as you are both concentrating intensely on the questions and answers.

If you feel you didn't get enough out of the session, ask to schedule another. Perhaps follow-up queries can be done on the phone.

Finishing Up

Barbara Walters likes to finish her interviews with a question something like this, "If your life were a screenplay, how would you write the plot line?"

Another common ending line is, "If you had your life to live over again, would you change anything?" When I asked Jonathan Winters this question, he became very serious and told me how much he admired Peter Sellers. Not because Sellers was such a great comedic actor but because he could bridge the gap to dramatic acting. Jonathan Winters, more than anything else, would like to be a serious actor.

Another standard ending ploy is to ask the subject to write his own epitaph. Writer Clifton Fadiman surprised me. I thought he would say something eloquent about his life with, what he calls, "those little hieroglyphics that squiggle across the page." Instead he quickly responded, "Let it say— 'He paid his bills!' "

The Last Question

The last question must be an easy one. Don't end on a sour note. Leave the subject feeling good about the interview. After all, you may want an invitation to come back for a second session.

To end the interview, pause, look at your notes and say, "Let me see if there are any questions I missed." There is silence for the first time during the interview. The subject is thinking, "Did I leave anything out? Is there something else I wanted to say?" Then, you look up from your notes and ask, "Is there anything I haven't asked that you think should be included in this interview?" Many times there will be.

You may want to sum up by checking spelling, statistics or

dates—details you should *not* have interrupted your subject to ask about during the interview.

Finally, close the notebook, turn off the tape recorder, but don't leave too fast. You might get a last quote while sitting there relaxing or heading out the door, and it may be the best quote of the day. The subject is relaxed and feels good. The tape recorder is finally off and the session has been satisfying. (He or she feels he hasn't revealed any deep secrets, dark emotions or family skeletons).

That's the time to flip him one final, penetrating question. It's like Detective Columbo walking to the door, then turning and saying, "Uh, by the way . . ."

After the Interview Is Over

You feel relieved! The interview went beautifully. Locked in your tape recorder are dozens of fantastic quotes—just what you need to write a great article. But you still have a lot of work to do. As soon as you leave the interview, you should turn the tape recorder on and record your impressions of the meeting. What did the subject say that impressed you the most? What was the best quote you can remember? What were the surroundings like? Describe the space in which the interview was conducted. Describe the individual. Make all these notes immediately, as you will not remember the details a week later.

Transcribing the Tape

Here again, don't wait. Transcribe the tape within a few days of the interview, while a mental and visual impression of the interview is still fresh in your mind. To make the job easier, you can purchase an on-off foot pedal that connects to your tape recorder from an electronics store like Radio Shack.

Do a little editing as you transcribe. You are not required to transcribe every word you recorded. The odds are that some of the material is unusable. Listen carefully to the tape and you will realize what and what not to write down. As you transcribe, do a bit of creative narrative writing to set the scene, provide background, describe the interviewee's appearance, and so forth. Words create ideas, and ideas compute to phrases, then sentences that become part of your article. Write as you work!

Editing Quotations

Let's face it, we all speak terribly. We scramble our syntax, mess up our grammar, and abort our thoughts midway. If you transcribe the interviewee's quotes exactly as they are spoken on the tape, the speech patterns will be difficult to read and understand.

It's the job of the writer to take these fractured quotes and edit them into a readable form. That means *edit* without doing an injustice to the essence of the original quote. The writer can improve the subject's grammar, but that doesn't mean the writer can add any thoughts, substantive words, or key phrases that weren't said during the interview.

Some journalists state that they will not alter, edit or condense a quote. "If it isn't usable just the way the subject said it, then don't use it," they say. I'll agree to that only up to this point: if syntax and grammar are a clue to character, the quote can be written verbatim. Consistently bad grammar or amusing malapropisms can be character-revealing. Just don't overdo it, as it can become irritating to the reader. *Whatever you do, never take a quote out of context and change what the speaker meant.* Not only is it bad journalism and ethically wrong; it may set you up for a lawsuit.

Play it straight. Quote in context.

To Quote or Not to Quote

When writing an article in which you need authoritative quotes to enhance and add credibility to the text, use the ones that make positive or interesting statements. The reader isn't going to be enthralled with quotes that begin, "Well, let's see, I was born on . . ." or "Yesterday I took my grandson to the circus . . ." when the person quoted is *the* expert on toxic waste.

Don't use *too* many direct quotes or the article will read as though your interviewee wrote it. Many of the ideas expressed by the expert can be blended into your narrative writing.

If you are writing a personality profile the text will be about half and half: half direct quotes, half narrative. How do you decide what to quote? The most brilliant, clever and incisive answers go in quotes. When you review the transcribed tape, circle the really good ones. Most of the background material, the exposition and the life history can be told in the writer's narrative. For instance, this is how I wrote about Julia Child in a 3,000-word profile called, "Lunch With Julia."

First the quote:

> "By age thirty-four I could barely boil water. I don't think I was a born chef, but I've always been hungry," Julia says, slicing the last of the smoked ham. "And I married a man who likes to eat. We both shared a passion for food."

Now, a bit of narrative:

> Julia McWilliams and Paul Child met during World War II in Ceylon (now Sri Lanka). Paul, a confirmed bachelor at age forty-two, was designing war rooms for Lord Mountbatten, and Julia was serving as a filing clerk in the Office of Strategic Services (OSS).

Now, another quote:

"I joined the OSS with every intention of becoming a spy," Julia remembers.

See how it works? A mixture of quotes and narrative, all of which were taken from the actual interview, makes the profile come alive.

Let's end this chapter with a quote. When asked why he never ran for government office, Jimmy Stewart replied, "Ah . . . waal . . . I don't talk fast enough to be a politician."

Now, that's quotable.

Titles That
Tantalize

I have never been a title man. I don't
give a damn what it's called.

—John Steinbeck

Fortunately for Steinbeck, *Grapes of Wrath* came to mind.
Gone with the Wind was far more poetic and dramatic
than Margaret Mitchell's working titles, *Tomorrow Is Another Day* and *Tote That Weary Land.*

The Great Gatsby grabbed the reader's attention quicker than
some of the titles F. Scott Fitzgerald first considered: *The High-
Bouncing Lover* and *Among Ash-Heaps and Millionaires.*

*Everything You Always Wanted to Know About Sex, but Were
Afraid to Ask,* is a bit long, but the book became a smash bestseller.
(It had originally been rejected several times under the title *The
Birds and the Bees*.) How about Robert Fulghum's 1989 smash hit,
All I Really Need to Know I Learned in Kindergarten, and Jonathan
Winters' book of short stories, *Winters' Tales.* All excellent titles.

Yes, tantalizing titles sell.

Now that you have finished writing your article or are well into your book, it is time to work on one of the most critical elements in selling it—coming up with a perfect title.

Editors look at titles as the hook that moves the reader into the body of the article or book. In a short piece the writer may have less than ten seconds to snare the reader's attention. A title like "Snakes Are Interesting" isn't going to grab anybody. "Snakes Alive!" has a far better chance.

Spend some time on your title. Title testing has shown that an excellent title alone will sell 15 percent more books. A great title, such as *Real Men Don't Eat Quiche*, can make a book into a bestseller. (And spawn sequels such as *Real Women Don't Pump Gas*.) Think of the title as the single most important piece of promotional copy you can write.

One of my nonfiction students wrote a camping story and titled it, "Camping in the Woods." Hardly a smasher. The story wasn't much better, just a dry rehashing about her and her husband's love of camping, something that had been written hundreds of times. Same old slant.

However, halfway through, I came across something that intrigued me—the word, "wok." She mentioned that she always took a Chinese wok along to use as a cooking utensil. There it was! The fresh, new slant the article needed: cooking with a wok on a camping trip.

The writer rewrote the article with this concept as the focus and included several wok recipes. After reading the untitled article to the class, I asked if anyone had any title suggestions. Here are two the class came up with:

"A Wok in the Woods"

"A Wok on the Wild Side"

The article sold.

Another student, infatuated with unicorns, wrote an excellent article on the subject. Unfortunately, the story idea had been done many times before and the odds of selling it, no matter how well written, appeared remote. It needed a hot title. The writer came up with this:

"Never Leapfrog a Unicorn"

A title can even generate a complete article. I found the phrase, ". . . speak softly and carry a lipstick," while reading a woman's magazine. I shared it with my class and two student writers came up with articles using that title. One was a story on feminism, the other on makeup.

The Purpose of the Title

The title can do two things: 1) hook the reader and 2) provide the slant.

The title, "A Wok in the Woods," not only gets the reader's attention, but tells what the article is about. Including the slant in the title is not a requirement. If the meaning of the title is obscure, you may want to add a subtitle, an enlightening after-thought that clarifies what your article is about. A self-explanatory title, such as "Rubber Boat Rafting Down the Colorado River," does not need a subtitle. However, if you have a title like "Static," you may need a subtitle: "The Effects of Sun Spots on Radio Waves." The title, "Dizzy," could be misleading without the sub-title, "New-Wave Dancing."

The Working Title

Before you begin writing, center a working title on the page and add your byline below it. This makes the project look official. It will also keep your article on target.

The working title may change as you write. A word or a phrase in the text may suggest a better title.

When I wrote the Devil's Island story used in chapter six, I made a list of titles to choose from:

"The Green Hell"

"The Wayward Paradise"

"The Disrupted Paradise"

"One Hell of a Paradise"

"Paradise Lost" (I knew I couldn't use that one!)

"The Dry Guillotine"

The title and subtitle I selected was: "Devil's Island: The Green Hell."

Giving your manuscript a working title will also get the creative juices flowing and keep them flowing. E. L. Doctorow said,

> You'll find a title and it'll have a certain excitement for you; it will evoke the book, it will push you along. Eventually, you will use it up and you will have to choose another title. When you find the one that doesn't get used up, that's the title you go with.

Can't think of a title? Then put "Untitled" on the first page and begin typing. That's the way Tennessee Williams did it. "The title comes last!" he would say. Even then, Williams spent some time mulling over exactly the right title. He changed *The Poker Night* into the classic, *A Streetcar Named Desire*.

Hemingway rarely tacked on a title while he was sweating out a new novel, preferring to research that task after the book was finished. In Hemingway's case it worked fine. *For Whom the Bell Tolls* and *A Moveable Feast* are cases in point.

Researching Titles

If you're looking for a book title, first check *Books in Print*, and *Forthcoming Books* at the reference desk in your library. No, not to "steal" a title, but to see if the one you're considering has been used. Of course, you could use the same title, but that would be counterproductive. *Books in Print* entries are listed by author, title and *subject*. That's a point worth noting. If the first word of your title defines the subject matter, your book will be easier to find in library listings.

Title and Copyright

What should you do if you see a title in a magazine that exactly fits what you want to say? Don't hesitate. Copyright law places titles in the public domain, which means any number of writers use them. If titles were copyrighted, editors would soon run out of titles. There are over 10,000 magazines in America, each publishing four to eight feature articles per month. The odds of a reader seeing or remembering a reused title are slim.

Short or Long Titles?

Editors suggest that the main title should not be over seven words. Even Robert Fulghum, whose ten-word titles, *All I Really Need to Know I Learned in Kindergarten* and *It Was on Fire When I Lay Down On It*, became bestsellers, admitted that his titles were too long. "No one could remember the names," Fulghum said, "so people referred to them as that 'kindergarten thing,' or that 'fire' book. I decided to release the third book with a short, easily remembered title: *Uh-Oh*."

Short titles, even one-word titles, are popular. The problem is thinking up a single-word title that fits what you are trying to say. Stephen King may have accomplished this aim with *It*, but a title like "Food" or "Money" is too vague. A good one-word title with a subtitle can be a good solution. Syd Field's book, *Screenplay*, is an example. The subject is clarified with the subtitle, "The Foundations of Screenwriting."

Using Word Play to Develop Titles

One of the surest ways to develop a catchy title is to slightly alter or rearrange the words of a well-known existing title, saying or cliché. Here are a few examples:

"This Spud's for You" (baked potato recipes)

"Rise and Dine" (sky-high restaurants)

"The Grill of It All" (barbecue cooking)

"Life Is a Cabernet" (red wines)

"The Pool is Always Bluer in the Other Yard" (maintaining a home swimming pool)

"Dome Sweet Dome" (football stadiums)

"Weed It and Reap" (gardening)

"For Heat's Sake!" (furnace maintenance)

"There Arose Such a Clutter" (garage sales)

"Have a Nice Chardonnay" (white wine)

"I Left My Fat Behind" (dieting)

"Clutter's Last Stand" (subtitle: "How to Dejunk Your Life!")

"How to Cook His Goose" (wild game cookbook)

"Women Who Munch Too Much" (eating disorders)

"My Old Unlucky Home" (nostalgia)

"Whittle While You Work" (exercise while doing housework)

"The United *Tastes* of America" (Big Macs in Europe)

"A Nose by Any Other Name" (plastic surgery)

"The A-B-Zzzz of Snoring" (cures for snoring)

"Through the Cooking Class" (basic recipes)

"Easter Eggheads" (decorating Easter eggs)

Another helpful technique in developing titles is to use alliteration (the repetition of the initial sound in two or more words of a phrase). Here are some examples:

"Kids, Kisses and Kindergarten" (getting children ready for the first day of school)

"Thin Thighs in Thirty Days" (There are a lot of exercise books!)

"Greats and Ingrates" (famous people)

"Bunetics—How to Have Better Buns" (We're not talking about baking)

The Advertising Method

How does the advertising industry attract attention to products? By using eye-catching techniques. You can apply the same technique to your title search.

Use a number:

"Ten Steps to Better Your Car's Gas Mileage"

"Five Ways to Increase Your Earning Power"

Ask a question:

"How Would You Like to Make a Million Dollars and Travel the World Free?" (A book or article on becoming a travel agent.)

"Did You Know You Can Stop Smoking?"

Use buzz words like "improve" and "new":

"Improve Your Golf Score!"

"New Ways to Make Pasta Dishes"

Offer the reader something beneficial:

"You Can Earn $500 a Week at Your Dining Room Table"

"Looking Great!—Without Diet or Exercise"

Title Punctuation

Most titles are sentence fragments and, as such, don't need closing punctuation. Eliminate the period at the end:

"Self-Publishing Your Book"

However, if the title asks a question, it must end with a question mark:

"Can You Achieve Your Goals?"

Use an exclamation point for emphasis:

"Great Guns!"

A subtitle can be introduced by a colon:

"Makeover: Makeup for Today's Woman"

Or by a dash:

"Sherry—The Golden Wine of Spain"

You can type the title and subtitle on the same line, as shown above, or add the subtitle on the next line:

SHERRY

The Golden Wine of Spain

Use upper case or lower case as you like. Underline the title if you think it looks better. However, within the text of a typed manuscript, a book title is always underlined (so that the typesetter can italicize it in the printed copy), and a magazine article title is set in quotation marks.

The first letter in a proper noun is capitalized, but most conjunctions (and, but, or, if, when, as) articles (the, a, an) and short prepositions (of, by, on, to, into) are not:

"The Art of Interviewing"

"Writing and Selling the Personality Profile"

If you are unsure, type the whole title in CAPITAL LETTERS and let the editor figure it out. The myriad rules for capitalizing titles can be confusing, but there are several good style manuals available, such as *The Chicago Manual of Style,* and *Words Into Type*.

What's important to remember is that the *right* title, no matter how it's punctuated, will entice the editor and increase your chance of a sale.

As Raymond Chandler once said, "A good title is the title of a successful book."

3
How to Sell

WHAT YOU WRITE

Selling Your Articles

If you do not write for publication,
there is little point to writing at all.

—George Bernard Shaw

The Query Quandary

There are two ways to sell a manuscript: first by submitting the
completed article to a magazine, and second by writing a query
letter asking an editor if he would like to see the manuscript. Due
to the volume of mail received—major magazines like *Redbook*
and *Reader's Digest* get over 30,000 unsolicited manuscripts a
year—magazine editors prefer query letters. More and more editors
today *require* them.

A query letter can also be advantageous to the writer for three
reasons:

1. A query letter will get read sooner than a manuscript. What
   mail do you think an editor reads first? Not that huge stack
   of thick manila envelopes on the corner of his desk. He
   goes for the business envelopes—the query letters. Editors
   take an average of two months to return a manuscript;

responses to query letters take them an average of two weeks.

2. *A query letter saves you mailing time and effort.* It greatly reduces the administrative chore of packaging and submitting the manuscript over and over until you find a buyer, and saves the cost of photocopying, envelopes and postage. It may take you a year or more of mailings to sell an unsolicited manuscript.

3. *A query letter saves you writing time and effort.* Let's say you have a great idea for an article, one that will require a lot of research and writing. The problem is, you don't know which editor, if any, would be interested in your idea. Perhaps the magazines you'd like to submit it to have already published an article on the same subject, or are planning to. Or, as editors are quick to point out, "The idea does not suit our present needs." A query will quickly get you the feedback you need before you write the article, saving you the labor of trying to market it after it's written. Query several—perhaps five or ten—editors about your idea. If the response is good, *then* write the article.

(A word of caution: in the beginning of your writing career, you must hone your talents by writing, writing, writing. You can learn to be the best query-letter writer in America, but the proof of your abilities will be your ability to master the craft of writing nonfiction.)

How to Write a Query Letter

The purpose of a query letter is to convince the editor to look at your manuscript when it's complete. A well-prepared query letter sells the editor on your *idea* as well as on your *writing ability*. The letter should be single-spaced and not more than one page long. The idea is to get in and get out fast. Propose only one idea per letter. Editors are turned off by what they call "shopping lists" (more than one idea per letter).

STEP 1: THE LEAD

The first paragraph of the letter should start with a bang to arouse the editor's interest. Begin with a challenging, emotional, provocative or practical opening. If you have already written the article, you may want to use the lead, or the hook. What better proof to the editor of your writing ability than this brief sample of your writing? You can tell the editor that the lead is "the first paragraph from my article on. . . ."

Here's another method that editors have responded favorably to: attach the first page of the actual manuscript to the query letter. That way you can express your *idea* briefly in the letter, and prove that you can *write* the article with the sample page.

Here's an example of a *bad* way to start a query letter:

In the article I am proposing to write, I plan to deal with the growing trend toward multiple families in single-family dwellings and the resultant effects . . .

Boring . . . !

Here's another example of a lead from an actual query:

One day, if Brooks Firestone has his way, when you hear his name, you'll think of wine, not tires. Brooks, the grandson of Harvey Firestone, shucked his directorship of the tire company and became a wine maker.

"You could put our entire winery in one of Gallo's tanks," Brooks quips, "but our wine is good!"

This query sold the Firestone Winery story, titled "A Vintage Dream," to three magazines and was eventually included in a book on wineries.

If you don't have a jazzy lead for the query letter, then simply tell the editor what you have. Remember, in nonfiction it's the *idea* that sells an editor. Although the writing must be good, an

editor is willing to take extra time editing it as long as the idea is
enticing. If the lead paragraph of your query doesn't define the
idea and slant of your proposed article, then make a statement to
that effect: "This is a story about . . . ," or "The slant of the article
is. . . ."

An editor once told me, "If you can't do it cleverly, then just
tell me what you've got—in simple words. If I like the idea, I'll
ask to see the manuscript."

What turns editors off? They say they receive too many inept,
self-defeating proposals: women's subjects to men's magazines and
vice versa; ideas based completely on published research; queries
on topics the magazine never covers. You don't query an airline
magazine with a letter offering a story on "The World's Worst Air
Disasters."

Is there anything that cannot or should not be queried? Short
articles, such as essays, opinion pieces, and humor are generally
not queried. Articles two to four pages long fit nicely into a business
envelope. As for humor, it speaks best for itself. A humor editor
is unlikely to be intrigued by a query letter stating that "This is
the funniest thing you will ever read . . ."

STEP 2: TITLE AND PICTURES

Next, list the *title* of the article and the *number of words* in the
manuscript. Don't propose a 3,000-word article to a magazine that
uses 800–1,000-word articles. Advise the editor if you have *photographs* or *drawings* to illustrate the article. Editors of small magazines with limited staff resources (and money) prefer complete
word-and-picture packages.

STEP 3: CREDIBILITY

Finally, list any *writing credits*. If you don't have any, don't say
anything. The epitome of a neophyte writer is one who says, "I've
never been published before, but . . ."

If you have a particular *authority* or *expertise* for writing the
article, let the editor know. For instance, if the piece is about the

medical profession and you are a doctor, nurse, or hospital administrator, say so. Editors love experts who can write.

STEP 4: ENCLOSURES

There are several possible enclosures you can include with your query:

- *A SASE (self-addressed stamped envelope)*. This *must* be included with any manuscript or query letter.
- *Literary résumé*. A résumé may include not only published works, but your area of expertise, experience, and educational background. You can list writing courses you have taken, conferences attended, literary awards received.
- *Tear sheet*. This is an actual copy or photocopy of a previously published article. A tear sheet will show the editor your writing style.
- *Illustrations*. You can include a sample copy of photographs or drawings. There's no need to send the originals.

Here is an actual query letter:

Ted Kreiter, Editor
The Saturday Evening Post
1100 Waterway Boulevard
Indianapolis, Indiana 46202

Dear Mr. Kreiter,

Today, at age 78, Jimmy Stewart looks like he has just stepped out of a vintage Norman Rockwell painting. He still has the appearance of the gangling young actor with the distinctive voice (a mixture of corn syrup, stammer and pure fun) who arrived in Hollywood 50 years ago. Once described as the "most normal of all Hollywood stars," Jimmy Stewart has always been the "Mr. Nice Guy" in town, and "everybody's man" to a world of fans.

I interviewed Mr. Stewart in his Beverly Hills home and have written a 3,000-word personality profile titled, "Jimmy Stewart—Everybody's Man." In the interview he talked about his favorite movie, *(It's a Wonderful Life)*, his favorite costar (Grace Kelly), his favorite director (Alfred Hitchcock), how he feels about being labeled a "legend"—and how he would like to be remembered.

Please advise if you would like to see the manuscript.

I have written a book for writers about the interviewing process titled, *The Art of Interviewing*. A second book, *Santa Barbara Celebrities—Conversations from the American Riviera,* is a collection of 27 celebrity profiles. My articles have sold to such magazines as *Playboy, The Saturday Evening Post* and *Seventeen*.

Sincerely,

Enclosures:
SASE
Literary résumé
Tear sheet, profile of Jonathan Winters

Letterhead Stationery

If you're going to be a selling writer, you should have letterhead stationery printed that includes your name, address and telephone number. Major magazines usually respond to your submissions with a phone call. If an editor calls and says, "This is Janet Smith of *Good Housekeeping*," you can bet she *isn't* calling to say your manuscript was the lousiest piece she has ever read. Have letterhead envelopes and mailing labels printed. And, sure, why not? Business cards.

Letterhead stationery is a literary "I am" presentation. As such, should you put "Freelance Writer" or "Writer" on your stationery? Many editors scoff at the idea, saying it isn't necessary; the manuscript or query letter makes that statement. *But*, if it looks and feels good to you—do it.

How to Submit a Manuscript

If, after you have submitted your query (on your new letterhead), an editor asks to see the manuscript, a return letter will normally advise the writer to send the article "on speculation." That does not mean the editor is required to buy the article, but shows she is seriously interested. At this point the odds of selling the manuscript are good.

When submitting the manuscript, attach a cover letter that begins with this phrase, "Enclosed is the article (title) that you asked to see on speculation." State on the outside of the envelope that the manuscript is submitted "As per your request." You don't want it to end up in the slush pile with the unsolicited manuscripts. Although an editor will usually ask to see an article on speculation first, she may, if she *really* likes your idea, send a letter of agreement or a contract assigning you to write the article.

The Professional Way to Prepare Your Manuscript

You'd be surprised how many fledgling writers don't understand the basics of manuscript preparation. Editors receive manuscripts written in pencil on yellow legal paper, coffee-stained and dog-eared, packaged in grocery store sacks tied with string. Editors admit that if the manuscript isn't professionally submitted they will never get past reading the title. Your manuscript is your introduction to an editor. It's like handing him a calling card.

What occupies most of an editor's time? That's right—reading. And an editor is used to reading copy in a standard format. Here are what editors say are the telltale signs of an amateur:

- Handwritten manuscripts and cover letters
- Fancy typefaces, such as script
- Perfumed stationery
- Crossed out words, phrases or sentences
- Lots of misspelled words in the article or cover letter

- Grammatical errors
- Blank checks or cash enclosed for the editor to buy stamps and mailing envelopes to return the rejected manuscript

AT THE TOP OF YOUR FIRST PAGE

Writer's legal name   Number of words
Address   First Serial Rights
Telephone number   © Date, Writer's Name
Social Security number

Your Title Goes Here
by
Writer's Name (or Pseudonym)

Begin the first words of the manuscript one-third of the way down the page. The title and byline are centered above that. Double-space all manuscripts. Leave at least a one-inch margin on both sides and at the bottom of the page.

To begin a new paragraph, double-space and indent. It is not necessary to triple-space between paragraphs.

Make your typescript as neat as possible. Corrections should be clean, and there should be no strike-overs or crossed-out words. Use a good, dark ribbon (black only), white bond paper, 20-lb weight. Use either elite or pica type. Submit photocopies of the manuscript; originals are not required.

AT THE TOP OF EACH FOLLOWING PAGE

Title   Writer's last name—page 00

Never use the reverse side of the page.

Each page should be numbered either at the top or bottom. Type the title (abbreviated if more than a few words) and your last name at the top of each page. Manuscripts are submitted loose-leaf (paper-clipped, not stapled or bound) and pages can get misplaced if not identified.

A stamped, self-addressed envelope (SASE) *must* be included with each submission. If the manuscript is only a few pages, it may be folded to fit in a standard #10 business envelope. Any manuscript, regardless of the number of pages, can be sent unfolded in a large envelope.

Illustrations such as color transparencies (35 mm slides) should be numbered and captioned on a separate page. Write your address on each slide. Black-and-white 8 × 10 glossy photographs should be captioned on an attached sheet of paper.

Estimate the word count of the manuscript by averaging the count of two pages, then multiply by the total number of pages. A double-spaced typed page averages 250–300 words.

On the last page of the manuscript, after you write the last word, skip a couple of spaces and type "The End." You can also use the old newspaper telegrapher's symbol, "—30—."

WORD PROCESSOR SUBMISSIONS

Editors will accept computer printouts if they are "letter quality." Poor-quality dot-matrix printouts are shunned by most editors. Some new dot-matrix printers can produce acceptable letter quality output. Most computer paper is standard 20-lb weight bond and is acceptable. If you use a tractor feed, remove the perforated tabs on each side and separate the pages.

Do not use computer graphics to enhance the text. Editors prefer a standard typed page. If you want to italicize words, underline them. Do not "right justify" as it makes proofreading a page a tedious task.

The Cover Letter

If you are submitting an unsolicited manuscript a brief cover letter with your material is recommended, but only if you have something to say other than, "The enclosed manuscript is submitted to your magazine for publication." This is what should be explained in a cover letter:

1. State that you're submitting an article (and give its title) for publication.
2. State your authority or expertise for writing the piece, and anything special about it. Don't try to hype the editor about how great the article is.
3. List your writing credits (if any) and add a résumé.

Your cover letter should be typed, single-spaced, and accompanies your manuscript. It should be very brief and professional. Never apologize for your writing skills or try to push the editor into buying the article. Never plead with an editor by saying something like:

> I would really like to see my enclosed manuscript published in your magazine. I know it is not professionally written and it would probably help if I learned to type and spell, but would you please give it a chance, anyway?

Don't try for the sympathy vote:

> I anxiously wait to hear from you about my manuscript. Please be kind with your reply. If it's bad news, put it gently, because I have a weak heart.

Silly, you say? You'd be surprised how many letters editors get saying this kind of thing.

Be professional. If you submit your manuscripts in a professional manner, you'll have a better chance of having your work accepted for publication.

Selling Rights

FIRST SERIAL RIGHTS

This is the term to use when you are contracting to sell a magazine manuscript. "Serial" does not mean that the article will be published in installments. Libraries call magazines "periodicals" or "serials" because they are published in continuing editions. *First serial rights* means the writer is offering the editor the rights to publish the article for the first time in any periodical. After the article is in print, the *rights automatically revert back to the writer*. Perhaps a clearer terminology would be *first-time rights*, or simply *first rights*.

SECOND SERIAL RIGHTS

This term applies to reprints and offers the magazine an opportunity to print an article that has appeared in another newspaper or magazine.

ONE-TIME RIGHTS

This term can be used if the article has previously appeared in print (perhaps more than once). The editor has no guarantee that he is the first to publish the work.

ALL RIGHTS

Caution! A writer who sells an article to a magazine under these terms forfeits the right to use the material in its present form in another magazine or publication. If the writer signs a "work-for-hire" agreement (usually an assignment to write a story) he also signs away all rights. If a writer sells all rights, the compensation for a reprint of that article might go to the magazine that bought the original manuscript.

Negotiating Rights

The majority of magzines buy *first serial rights*, or *first North American serial rights*. However, there are a few—very few—magazines that buy "all rights." "All rights" would require that the editor send the writer a letter of agreement or contract specifically stating that those rights are being purchased.

If, upon acceptance of the article, the editor advises, "We buy all rights," you respond with, "Sorry, I am a professional writer and I only sell first serial rights." Most editors will answer, "Okay, just thought I'd try." If the editor will not relinquish rights, you should consider either running the other way or asking for more money. But remember, no matter how good the original money, you will never see another penny.

If you receive a form-letter contract *after* the work has been accepted, simply draw a line through the part that reads, "buys all rights," initial in the margin and return the contract. The odds of hearing anything more from the editor are slim. If you receive a payment check that states, "Endorsing this check constitutes acceptance of buying all rights," don't worry. Even attorneys are wishy-washy about whether this ploy is enforceable. Simply deposit the check in your bank account *without a signature* and the words, "For Deposit Only."

Reprints

After the article is published you can sell the manuscript to another publication as a reprint. Then to another publication—and another . . .

A writer must look at writing as a business. That means you may want to sell each of your manuscripts to more than one publication. If you first sell the article to a regional magazine or newspaper with a limited audience, then why not offer it to a different magazine with a different readership? If the idea has wide appeal it can sell to many markets.

A Jonathan Winters profile I originally wrote for *Santa Barbara Magazine* eventually sold to three other magazines. The piece was marketed to a military magazine, *Family* (Winters had spent three years in the marines and had a wealth of humorous anecdotes to tell about his military service), then sold to *Prime Times*, a magazine for retired credit union employees. The profile was finally bought by *The Saturday Evening Post*.

Does the article have to be rewritten before it can be marketed again?

The answer is—*no*. Magazines that accept submissions the second time around call them "reprints." Editors judge whether their readership has been exposed to the article, and if not, will buy it as a reprint.

Do I tell the new editor the article has been published before?

The answer is—*yes*. The second editor will realize that, if the article was written well enough to be published once, it deserves a second serious reading. In other words, it has been "screened" by the first editor. However, it must be remembered that some magazines do not accept reprints.

Can I rewrite the article and submit it as a new piece?

If you completely rewrite the article with a different slant, then that *new* article can be marketed as an original piece.

Copyright

Under the copyright law of 1976, a writer's copyright protection starts with the creation of the work. The moment a writer puts words on paper they are copyrighted in his name. Not each word, but the way the writer expresses his idea. The idea itself cannot be copyrighted. That's good news for all writers. If you see an article idea that interests you, there's nothing to stop you from researching and writing an article about the same idea so long as you write about it in your own words.

If you want, you can add a copyright notice to your manuscript. Put this information on the title page under your name and address. The copyright notice includes:

- The copyright symbol—© in a circle (which can be drawn)
- The year when the manuscript was first created, or the year of its first publication
- The name of the writer

This is the way the copyright notice will read:

©1990 Cork Millner

Magazine articles cannot be copyrighted with the United States Copyright Office. Books can. There is a $10 filing fee. For copyright forms and information write to:

> Information and Publications Section LM-45
> Copyright Office
> Library of Congress
> Washington, D.C. 20559

If you are concerned about potential copyright infringement of an unpublished article you're submitting, there are informal methods to protect your work:

- Mail a copy of your manuscript to yourself by registered mail. Don't open it after it is delivered. The stamped postmark is your proof that the work was created on or before that date.
- Give a copy of your work to a second person, asking him or her for a dated, signed receipt.

Multiple Submissions

More often than not, magazine editors are agonizingly slow in replying to your query letter or manuscript submission. Admittedly, many of the smaller magazines are understaffed and too many editors feel their priority is getting the magazine to press, not treating writers with tender loving care.

Unfortunately, it happens all too often that a magazine editor will fail to respond at all. A student who took my class sent me a copy of a magazine in which her article had been published. The writer told me she had sent the article with a cover letter in mid-June. After a ninety-day waiting period—with no word from the editor—she wrote a follow-up letter. "Still no word," she said, "until last Monday, when I received a copy of the latest issue featuring my article and a check for $300! My first sale, a byline and a check, all in the same package!"

What does this all mean? To avoid lengthy waiting periods, writers should use multiple queries (a query letter sent to more than one editor at the same time), and multiple submissions (a complete copy of the manuscript sent to several editors at the same time). It is a faster, more effective route to publication. How do editors react to multiple submissions and queries? Few like them. But many editors understand that it is a reasonable and necessary tool to enable the writer to market an article. A group of magazine editors were polled about this. Their replies varied:

Gentlemen's Quarterly (GQ): "We don't accept multiple queries or submissions. If a writer isn't sure what publication he wants to be writing the piece for, he shouldn't be writing it."

Esquire: "We do consider multiple queries, which we prefer to submissions."

Good Housekeeping: "We will consider multiple submissions, but prefer exclusivity. A writer making a multiple submission should state so up front."

Harrowsmith/USA: "No, we don't accept multiple submissions. Generic brands are O.K. for aspirin, not articles."

The Saturday Evening Post: "We do accept multiple submissions, because we understand the tight schedule most writers are under."

Modern Maturity: "We do not accept multiple submissions at any time. We do not deal with properties that may be selected and printed by other publications."

What is the final analysis? Should writers submit multiple queries and submissions? The answer is a resounding—YES! A multiple submission gets your work before several magazine editors immediately, ensuring prompt results on each article or idea.

Should the writer tell the editor what he is doing? The answer is a positive—NO! I once queried *California* magazine and several other editors about an article idea. At the bottom of the query I added this note: "I'm sure you will understand that, due to the timeliness of this idea, I have queried several other editors." *California* responded by saying how much they loved my idea, that it was "just right for their magazine," then added, "Because you sent it to other editors, we have to reject the idea."

An editor once offered me this advice: "There are three sets of rules in publishing: editor's rules, agent's rules, and writer's rules.

"Editor's rules say, 'Don't send out multiple submissions because they make me work harder.'

"Agent's rules say, 'Multiple submissions are okay for *me* to send out, but not for writers who are submitting to my agency.'

"Writers allow themselves to be intimidated by editor's and agent's rules and forget that they can write their own rules, including one that says, 'Yes, the best submission technique to sell my work quickly, efficiently and profitably—call it 'creative marketing'—is through multiple queries and submissions.' "

How to Market Your Manuscript

Here are the steps to follow to help you sell your manuscript without trying a query first:

1. Make a list of markets you want to submit your article to.
2. Make as many copies of your article as you want to submit.
3. Type a personal cover letter to each editor. Don't say it's a simultaneous submission.
4. Mail them *all* out.

Now you ask: What if more than one editor offers to buy the manuscript? Answer: Break out the champagne! After drinking the bottle of bubbly you can do one of two things:

1. Write two different articles with different slants and sell them both.

2. If there is no way you feel you can write two articles, then choose the magazine that either pays the most or is the most prestigious and accept that offer. Inform the other magazine that you have accepted a better offer. No, it won't put you on a publishing blacklist. True, the editor may growl for a moment, then get back to business and forget the incident.

Mailing the Manuscript

The editor's name, title and publication should be typed on the address label. Which editor on the magazine's masthead do you send the manuscript to? If an "Articles Editor" or "Feature Editor" is listed, address it to him or her. You can select someone other than the editor in chief, managing editor, executive editor (editors often pick their own titles) to mail the manuscript to, such as an associate editor or assistant editor. The mail might end up on an editor's desk faster if he or she is on a lower rung of the editors' ladder.

Use first class mail if the manuscript is less than ten pages long and can be sent reasonably at current rates. If you are sending a heavy manuscript, it can be sent special fourth class at one low rate for the first pound. However, it may take longer to get to the editor.

As mentioned before, always include an SASE. In lieu of that, you can include a stamped self-addressed *postcard*. Advise the editor in the cover letter that the manuscript can be tossed out and the postcard returned. It will cost you, the writer, more in photocopies but will save on postage. It will also make everybody's— yours and the editor's—administrative chores simpler.

A stamped self-addressed postcard can include the following options:

Date:

Dear editor:

Please use this postcard to reply about the status of my manuscript titled _____:

1. _____Yes, we wish to buy your manuscript.
2. _____We are considering your manuscript and will get back to you within _____weeks.
3. _____Sorry, the manuscript doesn't suit our present needs. As you requested, we are returning this postcard in lieu of the manuscript.

Signed:

Negotiating the Price

You sold it! An editor sends a letter saying the magazine wants to buy the article. The offer is $250 for the manuscript. Not a lot of money, you think. But, it is a sale, perhaps the first one, so you accept the $250. Still, the question nags at you: Should I have asked for more? The answer is—*yes*.

Early in my writing career, I sent an unsolicited manuscript to a small trade magazine that paid in the $100–$300 price range. After two months without receiving a response, I sent a follow-up letter asking if the manuscript had been received. No reply. Two months later I sent a second follow-up letter stating I was withdrawing the manuscript from consideration and submitting it elsewhere. Still no reply. A month later, I saw a copy of the magazine on the newsstand, thumbed it open, and to my surprise saw my article with my byline. I contacted the editor saying I was ready to "negotiate the fee." The editor apologized for the oversight in not letting me know that the article had been accepting for publication and agreed to the maximum fee: $300. Having established a top rate of payment, I went on to write another half-dozen articles for the same editor.

Editors will rarely offer new writers their top fee. Yet they *will* pay it. "Tell your student writers that we expect them to negotiate the fee," I have been told by several editors. "We offer the minimum, but are willing to go higher."

If you have photographs or other illustrations, you may want to negotiate their sale separately, especially if one of your photographs is scheduled to appear on the cover. Most magazines have specific rates they pay for illustrations, while small magazines prefer to buy the complete photo/writing package for one price.

Will you lose the sale if you try to negotiate? Hardly. Remember, the editor contacted you saying she wanted to buy your article. As long as your negotiating demands aren't outrageous, the editor will come to an agreement. If you have an agent to market your work, you can bet that agent will try to get a higher price. Which brings us to the next subject:

Do You Need an Agent to Market Your Articles?

If your name is Mailer or Michener, Krantz or Collins, you need an agent. If you're a beginning writer you don't need an agent for your magazine articles. Not only do you not need an agent—*you can't get one*. An agent gets 10 to 15 percent of a writer's fee. If you sell a magazine article for $100, that $10 or $15 isn't going to keep an agent out of the breadlines.

The beauty of it is that most magazine editors don't expect you to have an agent for article submissions. That's to your advantage—you can build your writing reputation. Then, when you're ready to sell a book, use those credits to get an agent to represent you.

Record Keeping

You must keep accurate records of the query letters you have sent and the manuscripts you've submitted. Each writer can develop his own accounting method, but here are some ideas that may work for you.

SUBMISSIONS LEDGER

Such famous writers as Jack London and F. Scott Fitzgerald kept running entries in a ledger of what they had submitted and the dates when their manuscripts were either accepted or rejected. Such a ledger could look like this:

Date	Manuscript	Magazine	Accepted	Returned	Paid

3 × 5 CARDS

In addition to the ledger, it's a good idea to keep all corespondence relating to each manuscript together in a manila folder. Attach a 3 × 5 card with a paper clip to a copy of the manuscript and the succeeding letters sent or received. On the card keep a running account of the fate of the manuscript.

SPAIN'S PARADORES				
Date	Magazine	Accepted	Returned	Paid

At least once a month review the ledger and the 3 × 5 card for each manuscript. If you have not heard from an editor after two months, send a follow-up letter asking if the manuscript was received. If there is still no reply, follow up in two months with a letter or telephone call. If you don't receive a satisfactory response to this inquiry, send a letter stating that you are withdrawing your article from publication by that magazine. Keep a copy of each letter you write in the folder for that manuscript.

Once you have completely withdrawn a manuscript from publication, either because you have sold it or because you no longer feel that it's saleable, store it in the file folder. You may want to market it in the future. I once decided that a piece I'd written on a festival in Valencia, Spain, was not marketable after six rejections, so I filed it. A year later I got it out, looked it over and decided it *was* good enough to sell. I sent it to *Playboy* and they bought it!

Beating the Rejection Blues

"Sorry, your manuscript does not suit our present needs."

Those are the words, usually on a form rejection notice, that send writers into despair.

How can you cope with rejection? Simply by realizing that it's part of the creative process. I have received hundreds of rejections from editors and publishers. All writers have.

Irving Stone's *Lust for Life*, a biography of Vincent van Gogh, was turned down in 1934 by seventeen leading New York publishers, always with more or less the same comment: How can you sell a book about an unknown Dutch painter to the American public in the middle of the Depression? Irving Stone persevered and eventually sold the book.

What should you do about rejection?

- *First: Don't take it personally.* The editor is not rejecting you, or even necessarily rejecting your writing. It was your non-fiction *idea* that didn't suit the magazine's present needs. Keep trying until you find a magazine that it *does* suit.
- *Second: Keep more than one manuscript or query letter circulating.* If you received a rejection notice, there is still another manuscript out there ready to catch an editor's eye.
- *Third: Learn from your rejections.* Ask yourself why it was rejected. Was it the right idea for the magazine you submitted it to? Obviously, a bullfight story isn't going to appeal to a horse lovers' magazine.
- *Fourth: Don't expect personal replies from editors.* Editors receive too many manuscripts to reply with a personally penned letter. Occasionally, they *will* reply. (Alex Haley, author of *Roots*, says that one of the memorable moments in his early writing career was the day he received a rejection letter in which the editor had penciled in the notation, "Nice try!")

With all of this in mind, you will be able to accept the fact that no rejection you receive is likely to be especially kind. Certainly none is likely to match the rejection note that, according to the *Johannesburg Financial Mail,* a writer received from a Chinese economic journal:

We have read your manuscript with boundless delight. If we were to publish your paper it would be impossible for us to publish any work of a lower standard. And as it is unthinkable that, in the next thousand years, we shall see its equal, we are, to our regret, compelled to return your divine composition, and to beg you to overlook our short sight.

The Magazine Marketplace

Sir, no man but a blockhead ever wrote except for money.

—Samuel Johnson

'm going to send it to *Ladies' Home Journal!*" the student writer said. Then she looked at me for approval.

"Sure, it's worth a shot," I replied, knowing that her chances of acceptance were slim. Over the years I have told my classes how difficult it is for a new writer to market a manuscript with a major magazine. The "biggies," such as *Ladies' Home Journal, Good Housekeeping, McCall's, Parade, National Geographic, Playboy,* and *Reader's Digest,* each receive 25,000 to 40,000 unsolicited manuscripts a year. With competition that fierce, major national magazines are a tough market to break into.

But she was determined. "I'm going to send it to *Ladies' Home Journal.*" Her 1,000-word article, a warm, emotional story about her maturing 12-year-old daughter, was well written, but the *Ladies' Home Journal?* She'd already had the same article rejected by *McCall's* and *Redbook.*

One month later she called me.

"They bought it!" The words came breathlessly. "The editor

of the *Ladies' Home Journal* loved it! She said it was just right for their Mother's Day issue."

I was excited for her—a first sale, and to a major magazine! I asked how much the magazine had offered for the story.

"A thousand bucks!" she said. "A dollar a word!"

She had done it: gone against the odds and landed in the winner's circle. Then she told me, "The editor said my article was the first unsolicited manuscript they had bought in a year. They just happened to have a page open for a Mother's Day story and mine dropped across their threshold. Am I lucky!"

Luck. I've always liked Louis Pasteur's saying about luck: "Chance favors only the prepared mind." In this case the writer, true to Pasteur's word, had persevered and made her own luck. To make that luck work for you, you need to develop a marketing strategy.

I've seen too many good writers quit because they haven't been able to sell their manuscripts. Almost always they concentrated on the big publications and didn't look into a second, lesser-known group, the in-house or trade magazines, which comprise the majority of magazines printed.

I've had student writers sell to such national magazines as *Good Housekeeping*, *The Saturday Evening Post*, *Modern Maturity*, *TV Guide*, *Vogue* and *Bride's*, but I have had hundreds more sell to such not-so-well-known journals as *Rotarian*, *Amtrak Express*, *Webb Traveler*, *Discovery* and *Westways*. Many of these pay as well as the periodicals that are more familiar to the general public. What's important is that they receive far fewer submissions. Even more encouraging is that they are willing—no, let's say *eager*—to work with new writers.

The Major Classes of Magazines

CONSUMER MAGAZINES

These magazines—often referred to as "the slicks"—are the ones that can be bought through a subscription or at the newsstand by the general public. *Reader's Digest, Time, Sports Illustrated, Cosmopolitan* and *McCall's* are a few of these well-known magazines.

- *Pay scale:* They pay $2,500 to $4,000 for an article—enough to attract professional writers, the ones who have been in the business for decades and have made a name for themselves.
- *Quality of writing:* Editors prefer to work with writers who have produced high-quality material on earlier assignments. Editors like to have a stable of professionals they can call upon to develop the ideas generated by editorial needs. The competition here is intense. New writers *can* break in, and many do every year, but only when they show outstanding talent.
- *Staff-written:* Many articles published by consumer magazines are written by staff members. Some, like *Sunset*, are totally staff-written.

IN-HOUSE MAGAZINES

In-house magazines (also known as house organ magazines) are the best market place for new writers. There are hundreds of these lesser-known magazines, all in constant search of new talent.

In-house magazines have names like *Discovery, Westways*, and *Friendly Exchange*. In-flight magazines such as *TWA Ambassador, Sky Magazine*, and *American Way* fall into this category. These are magazines that are produced by business organizations and institutions. Some are written internally for employees, and others are produced for the general public.

Where do you find these magazines? You can't buy them on the newsstands or subscribe to them. But you can find them in hotel rooms, in the seat pockets on airlines, in magazine racks at doctors' offices, on shelves in credit unions and financial institutions, and on counters in military commissaries. Keep your eye open for them whenever you visit a business office. Here are a few in-house magazines:

Diversion	for the physician at leisure
Inn America	Holiday Inn's magazine
Regency	the Hyatt Hotel chain's magazine
Small World	for Volkswagen owners
Nissan Discovery	for Nissan automobile owners
Sky Magazine	for Delta Airlines
Friends Magazine	the Chevrolet journal
Discovery	for Allstate customers
Mature Health	arthritis information magazine
Prime Time	a credit union magazine
Privilege	for BankCard holders
Amtrak Express	the railroad magazine
Off Hours	for physicians
MD Magazine	another leisure magazine for physicians

These are only a few of the in-house magazines. There are thousands.

- *Pay scale:* The pay is not as high as most consumer magazines, but it can be surprisingly good—anywhere from $100 to $1,500.
- *Quality of writing:* Few of these magazines have staff writers or a stable of writers to which articles can be assigned. They depend on ideas in the form of query letters and unsolicited manuscripts from freelancers to fill their editorial needs. Instead of thousands of manuscripts each month, they may receive only a few hundred or a few dozen. The circulation of these magazines ranges from 100,000 to three million!

TRADE JOURNALS

There are also specialized magazines, called trade or professional journals, designed for people in specific fields or professions. Almost every occupation has its own trade publication. Farmers, teachers, construction workers, nurses—everyone who is employed—can learn more about their field from what they read in trade publications. Trade journals have names like:

Cashflow	Coordinated Capital Resources, Inc. for treasury professionals
Signcraft	for sign artists and commercial sign shops
American Trucker Magazine	for professional truck drivers
Air Line Pilot	for professional flight crews
Bookstore Journal	for the Christian bookselling industry
Roofer Magazine	for the roofing industry
American Bee Journal	for beekeepers

You may balk at writing for magazines with names like *Chain Saw Age* and *Fertilizer Progress*, but they are part of an open marketplace, one that is constantly looking for writers.

- *Pay scale:* The pay—$15 to $150 per article—isn't great, but writing for trade journals will establish your credibility and teach you how to work with editors. It's a great place to get started! If you have had training or experience in a particular occupation, you might consider writing for these magazines. I know a sign painter who submitted a humorous article to *Signcraft: The Magazine for the Sign Artist and Commercial Sign Shop*, sold it, and was asked to write a monthly column for the magazine. Trade journal editors love to discover new writers.

SPECIALTY PUBLICATIONS

These are consumer magazines, sold in bookstores and available in libraries, that are published for specific audiences, such as bicycling enthusiasts, horse lovers and karate experts. There may be dozens of magazines in each category, and each is a fertile marketplace for the writer who has an interest or expertise in that area. A woman in my class had a black belt in karate and decided to write for martial arts magazines. She unearthed twenty-nine magazines and newsletters devoted to the subject of self-defense. I've had other student writers who targeted such magazines as *Scuba Times, The Active Diver's Magazine,* and *Sports Fitness* and made quick sales.

Here are a few of the many other categories of specialty magazines: horse and rider; health and fitness; religion; retirement; sports; hobbies and crafts; computers.

Pay scale: The pay is small, somewhere in the $100 to $300 bracket, but if you have the expertise to write for one of these magazines it's a great way to break into print.

Quality of writing: Although the editors of these specialty magazines want well-researched articles by knowledgeable writers, the competition is less intense. Editors take the time to work with new writers.

REGIONAL MAGAZINES

Many times a writer's best publishing opportunity is in the hometown newspaper. Feature editors are constantly searching for interesting local stories. The pay won't get you a Rolls-Royce, but it will get you a byline and add to your résumé.

Hometown newspaper editors need feature articles on local personalities, regional events and special city programs. They need travel pieces, food articles and restaurant reviews. And the list could go on and on, because newspapers devour, on a daily basis, a wealth of words. You may have the expertise to write a column, perhaps one on gardening, health, antiques, cooking—anything that would appeal to a local readership. When a Santa Barbara writer, whose hobby was preparing gourmet dinners, heard that the local newspaper's cooking editor was leaving, the enterprising amateur quickly applied to do the column. The editor, who didn't want to hire a full-time reporter, accepted the freelancer. Since that time the writer has written a weekly cooking column profiling a local cook. You could try the same idea on your local newspaper editor.

- *Pay scale:* Local newspapers pay $0 to $50 for an article. Major newspapers such as the *New York Times* or the *Los Angeles Times* offer $100 to $250 for feature pieces such as travel stories, book reviews or opinion essays.

LITERARY MAGAZINES

Magazines in this category include university quarterlies and independent journals of poetry, fiction and commentary. *Amelia Magazine, December Rose, Golden Isis, Kaleidoscope* and *Prairie Schooner* are a few.

- *Pay scale:* Many times these magazines pay in copies or prizes. Literary magazines are a marketplace for the dedicated writer who views writing as an art rather than a business.

A Marketing Strategy

Let's say you have written, or are planning to write, a personal-experience article about trekking to Machu Picchu, the ancient Inca city in Peru. Ah, you say, a perfect idea for *Travel & Leisure* or *Travel/Holiday* magazines. But both are tough marketplaces. Travel magazines are used to working with a cadre of well-journeyed travel writers—names they already know. The odds of rejection are high.

How about your local newspaper? Most have a travel section. Send in the manuscript. The odds are good that it will be published. Then, after it has been published, you can try for that tough market. That's right—*now* try to market the article to *Travel & Leisure* or *Travel/Holiday*.

Remember what we said in chapter ten? *Yes, you can sell your article again—and again—and again*. Once the article has been published, the copyright automatically reverts back to the author. The exception would be if you signed a contract with the publication selling all rights, and, as noted, few magazines buy all rights. Regional publications won't bother with the paperwork.

Here, then, are the two routes you can take to selling your story:

> *Route #1:* Sell to a "low-road" market, such as a regional magazine, then work your way up to a high-road market by reselling to a major market. Your odds of rejection are far lower if you take this route, and besides, the piece will be edited for you by the regional editor. The next time out it will be a better article.

> *Route #2:* Sell the first time out to a major market. This is not easy if you haven't worked with the magazine's editor before. The odds of rejection are high. But even knowing that, you may still want to give it a try. If the piece happens to hit— hurray! If not, you can still take the lower road and sell to an in-house magazine or regional publication.

Either route will get you there. Route #1 is usually quicker and has far fewer bumps and curves.

Magazine Listings

Listings and addresses for magazines can be found in the annually updated *Writer's Market*. This research book lists 4,000 places where you can sell your writing and gives helpful hints for breaking into each market.

The Writer's Handbook is another good annually-revised research book. It lists 2,200 magazines where you can sell your articles, and has 100 how-to chapters on all fields of writing.

Another good source at the library is the *Literary Market Place*

(LMP) an annual publication listing everything from agents to book publishers to magazine editors. Additional resources are *The IMS Ayer Directory of Publications*, *The Gale Directory of Publications*, *The Standard Periodical Directory*, and *Ulrich's International Periodicals*.

Both *The Writer* and *Writer's Digest* magazines have monthly listings of new or active article markets.

How to Read a Market Listing

Here is a listing for a magazine titled *Friendly Exchange* that appeared in the *Writer's Market*. Let's analyze the terminology:

> FRIENDLY EXCHANGE. Meredith Publishing Service. Locust at 17th. Des Moines, IA 50336. Editor: Adele Malott. 85 percent freelance-written.

What does "85 percent freelance-written" mean? First, it means the editors have a small staff and have to generate much of what they print from ideas submitted by freelancers. It must be remembered that many of the writers in that 85 percent have worked for the magazine before. Still, it is open to new writers.

> QUARTERLY MAGAZINE. Designed to encourage the sharing or exchange of ideas, information and fun among its readers. For young, traditional families between the ages of 19 and 39 who live in the area west of the Mississippi River and North of Ohio. For policy holders of the Farmers Insurance Group of companies.

There you have it: an in-house magazine put out by Farmers Insurance Group for its policyholders. You won't find this one on the newsstands!

What if the listing mentions the magazine's circulation?

Circulation 4.5 million.

That's as much as *McCall's* and *Redbook* combined! Not a bad magazine to carry your byline.
What if the listing mentions payment terms?

Pays on acceptance.

A magazine can pay in one of three different ways:

1. *Pays on acceptance*. This means just what it says: the magazine editor will send you a check for your article as soon as he agrees to publish it. These should be the only terms under which a writer sells manuscripts. The American Society of Journalists and Authors will not recommend a magazine to its national membership unless the publication pays on acceptance.
2. *Pays on publication*. This term means that when the article is published the magazine will send the writer a check. But how long will that take? Six months? A year? What if the magazine decides a year later not to publish the piece? The writer is stuck. Look at it this way: when you walk out of a food store with a cart full of groceries, have you paid for them at the checkout stand? Of course you have; that's paying on acceptance. If you were to pay each time you consumed an item, that would be the same as paying on publication. Unfortunately, some magazines pay months *after* publication. Cashflow problems, they say. I'll bet the editor gets *his* paycheck, as does the secretary, and the telephone company and the electric company . . .
3. *Pays on pleading*. Occasionally a magazine is extremely slow to pay. Or simply refuses to pay. Your last resort is

to threaten to take the publisher to small-claims court. That will solicit payment—fast. I vividly remember the hassle I had with a consumer magazine. The publisher refused to pay. I sent letters, made telephone calls, even threatened small-claims court, all to no avail. Finally, I called the publisher's accountant, told my sad tale (even offered to take her to lunch) and asked for payment. The accountant laughed and said, "No problem. The check will be in the mail tomorrow." It was.

Anyway, back to our listing for *Friendly Exchange*.

Publishes an average of 5 months after acceptance. Offers 25% kill fee.

If you are writing an article on assignment for a magazine the editor will offer a kill fee, which is a percentage of the agreed-upon payment for the article. If for some reason the editor decides not to publish the finished article, the kill fee applies. A check for $250 on a $1,000-assignment is better than nothing, but it is still not an equitable amount for the time and effort you put in on the assignment. However, you *can* market the written piece to another magazine.

Buys all rights.

Obviously, the writer does not want to sell all rights. This can usually be negotiated down to first serial rights. (See Chapter 10.)

Submit seasonal/holiday material 1 year in advance. Simultaneous queries and photocopied submissions OK. Computer printout submissions acceptable. Reports in two months.

If you write a Christmas story for this quarterly magazine, then you should have submitted it last Christmas. Monthly magazines want seasonal material six to eight months in advance.

Reports in two months.

This means that the editor should have an answer—accepted or rejected—on your article submission within that time.

Sample copy for 9 × 12 SASE and five first class stamps; writer's guidelines for business-size SASE and 1 first class stamp.

This means that if you have not seen a copy of the magazine, you can send for one by enclosing a SASE (self-addressed stamped envelope). You can also get a copy of the magazine's "writer's guidelines," a rundown of what the periodical's editors are looking for in the way of articles, how much they pay, what rights they buy, etc. Here is an example of a "writer's guidelines." This one is from *Sky Magazine*.

1991 EDITORIAL GUIDELINES

DELTA AIR LINES

GENERAL OPERATING POLICIES:

SKY may best be described as a general-interest, national/international magazine with a primary editorial focus on business and management.

Its main purpose is to entertain and inform business and leisure travelers aboard Delta Air Lines with a varied mix of articles based on topics that have not necessarily been featured in other media. These guidelines, and the magazine itself, reflect that basic editorial direction.

In addition, *SKY* publishes what can only be accurately described as "substantive good news." This positive editorial orientation precludes any coverage or topics dealing with such areas as disease, disaster, sex, crime, politics, or other controversial aspects of contemporary life. In short, *SKY* discusses solutions—not problems.

Other submissions which **will not** be considered under any circumstances include: poetry, fiction, excerpted materials, cartoons, jokes, restaurant/hotel/events listings, previously published articles, religious, or first-person/experiential stories.

The publisher reserves the right to edit or condense a story, and also to augment a story with additional pertinent copy or photographs. All articles submitted to *SKY* or assigned by its editors must be original and, as law provides, may not be reprinted after publication in *SKY* without the express written permission of the publisher and the contributor.

SKY employs a format-development system that calls for planning of editorial content 6–9 months in advance of publication. In order of priority, general areas of feature coverage comprising the editorial mix in a typical issue of *SKY* are as follows:

Business: Industry trends, growth, and analyses; corporate techniques and methods of a topical nature; general subjects affecting, or of interest to, a business/professional audience.

Lifestyle: Leisure, recreation, design (architecture, etc.), personal health and appearance, Americana.

Sports: Professional sports according to season; major amateur and collegiate events; individual sports activities and fitness.

Arts & Entertainment: Film, theatre, music, TV, art and dance. (No reviews.)

Consumer: Contemporary trends as they affect the buying public, food topics, etc.

Technology: Computer technology, space travel, telecommunications and information processing, general scientific research and development.

Collectibles: Varietal items as seen from both a hobby/collecting and investment-oriented approach.

Leadership Profile Series: Almost exclusively focused on leading national and multinational CEOs; subjects determined by the airline at least 12 months in advance. No queries or MS accepted in this category.

Travel: Though *SKY* does not accept queries in this category—

primary destination features (generally one article per issue) for *SKY* are predetermined by Delta management 12 months in advance—writers interested in submitting travel features are advised to forward a list of destinations they are equipped to handle, for consideration when specific area needs, particularly international, arise.

Standard Columns & Departments: *SKY*'s columns and departments include Management, Behavior, Personal Finance, Language, and a crossword and puzzle page. Queries for these columns should be submitted in the same fashion as for regular features.

Expansion Stories: While the departments identified above are represented in *SKY* by assignments made according to formats determined several months in advance of publication, Halsey does maintain a catalog of stories to be on hand for expansion purposes. These stories, which are held for use when and if additional advertising pages necessitate expanding editorial content, fall into the same general categories as the standard departments. They should be timeless; not written so as to restrict use to any particular months or time of year; and consist of text/photo packages.

TERMS AND PAYMENT:

SKY pays on acceptance of manuscripts for assigned stories. Payment varies according to several factors (including regularity of contributions to the magazine), and naturally is higher for text/photo packages, but in general, compensation for assigned stories (1,800–2,000 words for features) ranges from $500–$600; for column material (generally 1500–1700 words), $400. Compensation for expansion stories is generally less than that for assignments. Kill fees of 100% are paid when cancellation of a completed assignment occurs through no fault of the writer.

SKY buys first North American rights only; and as a courtesy to contributors, extracts no fee for processing reprint/republication request from writers, photographers and artists.

The majority of the photography and illustrations used in *SKY* are full color. Most photography is provided by a stock photo house, as well as specific sources/contacts which writers are instructed to provide at the time of submission of an assigned manuscript. Artwork is prepared by independent illustrators with whom *SKY* works on a regular basis. Photographers and artists wishing to offer their services to *SKY* should contact the magazine's Photo Editor.

INVOICES:

Contributors should submit their invoices to the Editor, noting the article by title and the issue to which it pertains; and invoices should accompany assigned material when submitted. In the case of expansion stories, contributors will be notified if and when such a piece will be used, and thereafter, should invoice Halsey as above.

Long-distance telephone expenses are reimbursed, and certain other expenses may be approved for reimbursement, as well. However, prior approval by the Editor is necessary, and receipts or copies of bills must be provided for bookkeeping purposes.

DEADLINES:

SKY is distributed aboard Delta's aircaft at the beginning of each month. Copy is usually due 60 days prior to issue date.

The critical importance of deadlines cannot be overemphasized, and with our early assignment system (usually providing at least 45 days working time prior to deadline), there should be no excuse for broken deadlines. However, if at any time a problem arises which might lead to a broken deadline, contributors should notify the Editor immediately.

Contributors must be absolutely certain that all material provided is accurate and up to date. Facts, figures, people and places should be verified before submission. Substantiation may be required occasionally.

SUBMISSION OF QUERIES:

Although *SKY* employs a long-term format development system as previously cited, queries are invited in keeping with the departments and standards described in the Guidelines. Queries should be submitted to the Editor, in the following format:

Working Title

General Concept (100 words or less)

Approximate length of story

Description of accompanying visual components (unless a column)

Unsolicited manuscripts and queries *will not* be returned unless accompanied by a self-addressed, stamped envelope (SASE) to en-

sure a response and/or return of materials. **Publisher accepts no responsibility under other circumstances. Fax transmissions** *will not* **be considered. NO PHONE QUERIES ACCEPTED.**

SUBMISSION OF ASSIGNED MANUSCRIPTS:

When submitting manuscripts, the cover or title page should identify the story by working title; the author, with bio information; the address and telephone number of the author; the issue for which the story has been assigned, if an assignment; and the estimated length of the story, in number of total words.

Manuscripts should be keyed double-spaced on plain white paper, and contributors are urged to retain a copy for their files. Once accepted, manuscripts will not be returned. Floppy disc or modem transmissions are acceptable for **assigned** articles only.

Photographs must be accompanied by outlines of an explanatory and informative nature, and should be original slides or transparencies sized 35mm, 2¼″, or 4″ × 5″. Photographs should always be protected in plastic sheets or sleeves, and mailed with cardboard backings.

Patience on the part of those submitting materials for consideration is appreciated. Due to the heavy volume of material received, 30 days is our average response time.

What Magazines Pay

Here are examples of what various magazines pay:

$2,500 AND UP:

Connoisseur	*New Jersey Monthly*
Family Circle	*New Woman*
Glamour	*Omni*
Good Housekeeping	*Parade*
Home Mechanix	*Playboy*
Ladies' Home Journal	*Reader's Digest*
Mademoiselle	*Redbook*
McCall's	*Smithsonian*
National Geographic	*Vanity Fair*

$1,500—$2,000

American Legion   New York
Boys' Life   Parents
Elle   Philip Morris
Esquire   Psychology Today
GQ   Runner's World
Harper's Bazaar   Tennis
Health   Town & Country
Lear's   Working Mother
Modern Maturity   Yacht

$1,000—$1,400

Arizona Highways   Marathon World
Bon Appetit   Outdoor Life
Bride's   Personal Computing
Cosmopolitan   Popular Mechanics
Discovery   Seventeen
Forum   Skiing
Gold Digest   Sports Afield
L.A. Times Magazine   Travel & Leisure
Los Angeles   TV Guide

$750—$900

American Medical News   Kiwanis
American Way   Moneymaker
Chicago   Nation's Business
Creative Living   Off Hours
Diversion   Outside
Enquirer   Quill
Food & Wine   Rolling Stone
Hippocrates   Sports Illustrated
Home   Vermont Life

$500—$700

Amoco Traveler	*MD*
Amtrak Express	*People*
Emmy	*Snow Country*
Genesis	*Sport*
Home and Away	*Stereo Review*

$100—$400

Army	*Palm Springs Life*
Horse and Horseman	*Privilege*
Nissan Discovery	*Rotarian*
Off Duty	*Westways*

If you find the right magazine, your reward will not only be a byline but payment for your work. As author Dorothy Parker once said, "The most beautiful words in the English language are, 'Check enclosed.' "

Selling
Book Ideas

It circulated for five years, through the halls of fifteen publishers, and finally ended up with Vanguard Press, which, as you can see, is rather deep into the alphabet.

—Patrick Dennis on *Auntie Mame*

C an you name the all-time nonfiction big seller?

It's a book with more than 30 million copies in print! No, we're not talking about the Bible. We're looking for the title of a contemporary book. *Gone with the Wind*? Not even close. Remember, it's a *nonfiction* book.

The book? Dr. Benjamin Spock's *Baby and Child Care*. If you guessed Dale Carnegie's *How to Win Friends and Influence People*, you were close. It came in second on the nonfiction list.

How did these books make it to big-seller status?

Each had the right idea for its time.

Take Robin Norwood's *Women Who Love Too Much*. It hit the self-help bookshelves and spawned dozens of copycat books, many of which became bestsellers. Then there's *The One-Minute Manager*, *Real Men Don't Eat Quiche*, *Everything You Wanted to Know*

About Sex but Were Afraid to Ask and *All I Really Need to Know I Learned in Kindergarten*.

Each of these books had a unique idea, yet none would have appeared in print if the writers had not had a burning desire to write. Not one of the authors of those blockbusters had ever written a popular consumer book before!

Still, ask yourself: *How can I write a book? How can I write all those pages!*

The Mechanics of Writing a Book

A nonfiction book will average 50,000 to 100,000 words. (That's an average of 200 to 400 double-spaced manuscript pages.) There are many exceptions to this average-length book. A heavily illustrated book may only run 20,000 to 30,000 words. My first book on sherry wine was composed of 25,000 words and 100 photographs.

Other than having a big idea, what's the difference between writing a 5,000-word article and writing a 50,000-word book? Three basic things: 1) the time spent writing; 2) research and organization; and 3) revision.

TIME SPENT WRITING

Here's how Joseph Wambaugh, the author of such nonfiction books as *The Onion Field* and *The Blooding*, says it's done:

> First, you have to get rid of that terrible bugaboo that you have to fill all those blank pages. If you sit down and do four double-spaced typewritten pages a day—and you can do that—that's 1,000 words a day. You'll have a book in three to four months. That is, you'll have a rough draft.

The rough draft—that's the hard part. That's the one that will make you want to shove yourself away from your typewriter and cry out, "I don't need this job, my face is my fortune!" Just remember, those first pages are not only *rough* to write; they're a very *rough* draft. What you write at this early stage doesn't have to show great literary merit. Don't worry how bad a sentence, or a paragraph, or even a whole page may sound. Just keep writing. Push ahead! Get those thoughts, those ideas on paper.

The second draft will be a lot easier and take an additional three or four months. During the writing you will begin to see that sparkling light at the end of the tunnel.

The final draft is fun. That's right—*fun*. You can *see* the actual book coming alive in front of you. All you have to do is add the final creative touches.

So, how long does it take to write a book? Eight to twelve months. It took Michelangelo four years to paint the Sistine Chapel ceiling.

Now, you may ask yourself: Does writing a book require a better command of writing techniques? Am I *ready* to write a book? Somewhere I read that a person must write a million words before he can become a writer. Believe me, you can write a mere 2,000 words and become a *selling* writer. Sure, the more you write the better you're going to get at your craft. It would be nice to have a dozen or so magazine articles under your writer's belt to prime the old writing pump, but it's not necessary. Robin Norwood wrote only one magazine article (unsold) before she penned *Women Who Love Too Much*.

The only real question you need to ask is this: Is my idea broad enough in scope and do I have enough material to fill a book? If you figure you can only write 5,000 words, you had better settle on a magazine article.

RESEARCH AND ORGANIZATION

Unless your book is an autobiography, you will have to spend time gathering information. (Even an autobiography will require some research, as few people can remember the name of every product, every date, every personality they came in contact with during a lifetime.) Here's some research sources to consider:

1. Books with similar subject matter
2. Magazine articles on the same idea
3. Newspaper stories
4. Interviews with experts
5. Diaries and letters
6. Material from your own files, especially if the subject matter is in your area of expertise, such as case histories of clients

Once you have pulled together all this research material it is time to organize it into chapters.

First, make a rough outline of chapters with the information you want included in each. Many writers use 3 × 5 cards, listing the chapter number and each item that will go into that chapter. Cards may need to be rearranged to get the material in the logical order. During the writing, you may also want to reorganize the chapter sequence.

Since it is a nonfiction book you may not want to write the first chapter first. The subject matter of another chapter may interest you more, or you may feel it is easier to write. The idea is to begin writing, and not spend the rest of your life researching.

REVISION

You've finished your book and turned it in to your editor. You're through! Time to take an extended vacation. Just don't stay away too long. The book *will* require some revision.

Book editors offer the final objective input, and their creative ideas are invaluable. Your assigned editor will request revisions: You don't have to follow every suggestion an editor makes, but neither should you arbitrarily discard the comments. The editor isn't requesting revisions because she wants you to work harder, she makes them because she wants to publish the best book possible. Depending on the amount of revisions, the final editing will take you two weeks to two months to complete.

Evaluating Your Book Idea

Editors are the first to say they don't need a writer with a track record to make big money with a nonfiction book. What they need is a really different idea, a highly original, up-to-the-minute idea that will startle them into paying attention—and paying money. The idea must be provocative, exciting, controversial and loaded with human interest, a fresh, timely concept that will make people rush to the bookstore to buy a copy.

And you've got one, right?

First, ask yourself: Am I the first writer to come up with this idea? How can I tell if another writer hasn't already done it—or isn't doing it right now?

A good place to start is the bookstores. Take note of titles that are similar to, or suggest your idea. Take a look at *Forthcoming Books,* which details the books publishers currently have in the works. Research *Books in Print* to see if there are ideas and titles similar to yours. Finally, check catalogs of the publishers you intend submitting your proposal to. Catalogs can be obtained by writing to the publicity department, or by consulting the *Publisher's Trade List Annual* in your local library. Don't be surprised if you find a half-dozen books similar to yours. There are a lot of books in print! Don't be discouraged. Your idea is fine—as long as you have something new to say, or a way to say it differently.

Before you try to find a publisher, evaluate your idea by asking yourself:

- Will it appeal to a wide general audience?
- Do I feel strongly about my idea?
- Do I have the appropriate knowledge and expertise?
- Have too many other books been written on the subject?
- Can I bring a fresh new slant to an old idea?

You must be able to explain your idea in a single sentence—a statement of thesis. You won't be able to do this until you have a keen focus and have limited your book to a coherent, well-defined structure with manageable boundaries. If you need a full paragraph or more to describe your idea, you must narrow your focus. For instance, here's a well-defined book idea:

> *Making Faces* is a makeup and skin-care guide for the cosmetic klutz, the woman who doesn't know anything about the subject and can't figure it out.

How to Sell Your Book

What's the best way to sell your nonfiction book?

First: *do not* send a completed manuscript to an agent or publisher. Send a query letter or a book proposal.

THE ONE-PAGE QUERY LETTER

Before you start writing your book, you may want to send out a "feeler" to several agents or publishers to see if you can stir up any interest. A book query is a one-page sales pitch. It should include the following information:

- The focus, theme or *slant* of your book
- Why the book will fill a need
- The potential market for the book
- Your expertise on the subject
- Your publishing credits (if any)
- An offer (at the end of the letter) to send a detailed proposal

Here is a one-page query letter example:

June 1, 1990
John D. Short, Publisher
Fallow Books
211 Country Lane
Watershed, CA 93009

Dear Mr. Short,

THE ART OF INTERVIEWING is a new book that covers all aspects of the interviewing process and is an indispensable guide for writers who want to learn the art of questioning. By learning how to interview, the writer can:

Make Any Article Saleable

Getting firsthand, expert quotes, will beef up *any* nonfiction work and make it more saleable. Learning the interviewing process will enable today's creative writer to add vitality and credibility to a manuscript.

Write the Personality Profile

The writer can also learn to write one of the fastest-selling articles in publishing—the personality profile. A writer doesn't have to interview Harrison Ford or Kathleen Turner to sell a profile. Fascinating folks with unique lifestyles are everywhere. Editors from *The New Yorker* to the writer's local newspaper want to feature these people.

THE ART OF INTERVIEWING is a practical, step-by-step guide to interviewing, with chapters on:

- How to Get the Interview
- Preparing the Questions
- Conducting the Interview
- Writing the Manuscript
- Selling the Finished Article

The book includes personality profiles of Jimmy Stewart, Jonathan Winters and Bo Derek.

Potential market: In the United States there are an estimated two million writers, including professional writers, those pursuing a separate career while writing part-time and those currently learning writing skills. There are 40 magazines directed at writers, 850 annual writers conferences, and 120 writers organizations. THE ART OF INTERVIEWING is timeless and can remain on a back list for ten years or more.

*****

The letter closes with a brief list of the author's credits and the final sentence: *A detailed proposal and sample chapter are available on request.*

A query letter can be sent to as many agents and publishers as you desire. If you get positive responses from editors asking to see the book, then it's time to write the book proposal.

Writing the Book Proposal

Think of a book proposal as a sales brochure detailing the benefits of publishing your book. It should be designed to convince a publisher to make a substantial investment in your book because she feels she can sell it profitably.

A book proposal can be sent directly to a publisher by the writer or can be used by an agent to negotiate the sale. The success the writer or the agent has in selling the book depends to a large degree upon the quality of the proposal. Each agent has slightly different ways to organize a proposal, but for the most part, the essentials are the same.

A proposal is written in the third person, active voice, and present tense. It is typed, single-spaced with consecutively numbered pages. (Sample chapters will be double-spaced.) Book proposals vary in length. Some editors and agents prefer short proposals of four to five pages while others want lengthy ones of up to twenty-five pages. The proposal, plus a twenty-page sample chapter, can constitute a nearly fifty-page package. This sales package is broken into several elements and includes:

- Title page
- Proposal table of contents
- Book concept
- Marketing concepts
- Publishing details
- Author's background

- Outline of chapters
- Sample chapter or chapters

TITLE PAGE

This is a cover page for the proposal. Center the book's title one third of the way down the page, then double-space and enter the subtitle. Double-space again and type: A Book Proposal. In the lower right-hand corner add your name as the author.

The selection of your book title is of great importance and deserves careful thought. A title must convey an irresistible appeal to your readership. Try to keep your title short; seven words is considered enough. You may want to add a subtitle to convey the precise meaning of your book. (Refer to Chapter 9, "Titles That Tantalize.")

PROPOSAL TABLE OF CONTENTS

This is the *proposal's* table of contents, not the book's. List each section of the book proposal and the page numbers for easy reference. Here's an example:

Table of Contents

BOOK CONCEPT

This section, about two to five pages long, can be labeled "About the Book." Think of this major section as an expanded book-jacket blurb. When you pick up a book in a store, the first thing you look at is the cover. Then you turn it over and read the jacket, which is essentially a sales pitch. Study book jackets and you'll begin to see how to write yours.

Start with a hook to grab the editor's attention:

- State a startling fact
- Quote something compelling
- Use an anecdote

Once the proposal has hooked the publisher with a startling fact or compelling thought and has shown the need for the book, the rest of the *book concept* section must establish how your book satisfies that need. Follow the hook with a *synopsis of the book's contents,* and any *special features,* such as interviews, you plan on doing with experts.

MARKET

This is the place to explain why your book is better than or different from others published on the same or similar subjects. List current titles that might be competitive and say why your book fits a niche that these published books don't cover.

State who the book's particular audience is and how many potential readers are out there. Be specific. "Lots of people are waiting for this book to be published," is an empty superlative. Ask yourself *what* special groups will want to read your book. A writer in my class worked on a book called *Tips,* which was defined as "Helpful 'Tips' for restaurant managers, hostesses, waiters and waitresses." The writer contacted several major hotel and restaurant chains asking if they would subscribe to the book as a teaching aid for restaurant employees. The positive responses pointed up the sales potential of the book.

Under this marketing section also describe the category the book fits into: self-help, health, business, finance, entertaining, etc.

The publisher wants to know if you, as the book's author, are willing to promote the book. Make a statement something like this:

"The author is available to travel and make public appearances to promote the book and is more than willing to be a guest for radio and television interviews. The author will aggressively seek speaking engagements that promote this book."

PUBLISHING DETAILS

This section covers book specifications and projected delivery. State the projected word count and how many photos, illustrations, charts or graphs are available. Mention any "backmatter" you plan on including, such as an index (usually done by the publisher), bibliography, glossary of terms, etc.

Finally, provide a reasonable estimate of the amount of time you need to complete the book: usually six months to a year.

ABOUT THE AUTHOR

Biography: This is written in the third person: "John Jones is a professional therapist. . . ." Emphasize your authority for writing the book. Feature the area of expertise that enables you to write the book knowledgeably. Add writing credits (if any), literary awards, writing organizations you belong to and educational background.

OUTLINE OF CHAPTERS

This will take three to five pages. Give each chapter a title and write a few paragraphs of narrative detailing exactly what each is going to cover. Chapter titles are important. Give them as much thought as you did the book's title. Chapter titles, as well as the organization of the chapters, may change as you proceed with writing, but publishers recognize this as a natural part of the creative process. The chapter outline will not only help you organize your book, but will show the editor that you have a clear grasp of your subject and can present it in a logical progression.

SAMPLE CHAPTERS

Include one (or two) sample chapters to show your writing style. What you send does not have to be the first chapter. Send the chapter that best represents the book's concept. Whatever chapter you send, make sure it shows your writing at its best.

You may want to attach an appendix that includes relevant documents, such as press clips supporting your idea or credentials. You may want to enclose sample illustrations (photocopies are fine). If you have good reviews of previous books, include them.

Why Do Publishers Reject Book Proposals?

When asked why they reject book proposals, publishers offer the following reasons:

- Doesn't fit our requirements
- Dull, pedestrian, nonprofessional writing
- Imitative; been done before
- Unimportant idea

As you can see, the category, "Doesn't fit our requirements," heads the list. This catchall phrase can mean one of two things:

- The publisher has already done (or is currently doing) a book on the same subject
- The idea doesn't fit into publisher's catalogue

Study the publisher's requirements. It's a waste of time sending your book to a publisher who doesn't use that type of material.

Submitting Your Proposal

There are two ways to submit your proposal: 1) through an agent; or 2) directly to the publisher.

AGENT REPRESENTATION

An agent gets 10 to 15 percent of whatever fees the writer receives. That means an agent works for nothing, unless your book is sold. Is an agent worth the 15 percent? *Yes.* A book editor looks more favorably upon an agent-submitted book proposal than on one that comes directly from the writer. He knows that the book has been screened by a knowledgeable professional who believes in its market potential. An agent will not waste the editor's time on an unsaleable book.

An agent also understands book contracts and will try to get the best advance and the best terms for you, such as royalty percentage, subsidiary rights and paperback sales.

Some agents charge a fee ($50 to $250) just to read your manuscript. A fee is usually refundable if the agent accepts your manuscript for representation. Other agents will bill you for expenses, such as telephone calls and the postage spent to sell the manuscript.

A flyer that offers information about literary agents and lists some of them can be obtained by writing the Society of Authors' Representatives, Inc., 39½ Washington Square S., New York, NY 10012. Literary agent listings can also be found in the *Literary Market Place* (LMP) or in *Writer's Market*.

SUBMITTING DIRECTLY TO THE PUBLISHER

A writer can bypass the agent and submit the proposal directly to a publisher. Small presses state that anywhere from 30 to 90 percent of the books they publish come from material submitted directly by the writer.

Names, addresses and editors of *major publishers* can be found in the *Literary Market Place* (LMP).

The addresses of *small presses,* which now publish a wide variety of nonfiction, may be found in the *International Directory of Little Magazines and Small Presses,* published annually by Dust-books, P.O. Box 100, Paradise, CA 95969.

University presses publish books in specialized fields. For a complete list of these presses you can consult *LMP* or the Association of American University Presses, One Park Avenue, New York, NY 10016.

Advance against Royalties

No matter who publishes your book, you should be granted an advance against royalties. The advance is nothing more than survival money for the writer during the process of writing the book. Depending on the situation, and the wording of the publishing contract, it may be the writer's money to keep even if the publisher decides later not to publish the book. Of course, you have also guaranteed the publisher by contract that the book will be finished by a specific date or the advance must be returned.

The *advance against royalties* is the specific amount of money paid to the author by the publisher for the right to publish the book. It is generally paid in two installments: 50 percent upon signing the contract and 50 percent upon delivery of the final manuscript.

The *royalty* is the amount of money the writer receives for the sale of each copy of his book. Royalties above and beyond the advance are not paid to the writer until enough books have been sold to pay off (or "earn out") the advance. In other words, if you received a $1,000 advance against royalties, and were to receive royalties of $1 from the sale of each book, you wouldn't be paid any additional monies until sales passed 1,000 books. Royalties usually run from 7 to 12 percent of the book's retail price (sometimes of the book's wholesale price) depending on whether the book is published in hardcover or softcover. Usually the percentages are calculated on a sliding scale predicated on sales of the book. Here is an example of an author's royalty "schedule" from an actual contract for the sale of a hardbound book:

10% of the catalogue retail price of the first 5,000
copies sold in the U.S.;

12½% of the catalogue retail price of the next 5,000
copies sold in the U.S.;

15% of the catalogue retail price of all copies sold in
the U.S. thereafter.

The writer is also contracted to share other revenues with the
publisher, such as those from the sale of motion picture rights,
educational picture rights and foreign language rights. These shares
will generally run to 50 to 90 percent for the writer.

Most book sales for a new writer generate small advances: $500
to $1,000 from small presses and $2,000 to $5,000 from major
publishers. Any book in the $10,000-to-$50,000-advance bracket
is a big sale. (There are always exceptions: For his first novel,
Promises to Keep, which asked the question, "What if JFK had
survived the assassination?", George Bernau got a phenomenal
$750,000 advance.) The more the publisher advances, the greater
effort he will expend in marketing the book. That's good for everyone—especially the author.

Self-Publishing

Self-publishing—I prefer to call it "independent publishing"—
has become a popular option for writers. There are certain advan-
tages to publishing your own book:

- *Publishing time:* It takes a publisher anywhere from a year
  to two years to publish your book *after* the contract has been
  signed. A self-published book can be off the printing press
  in three to six months.
- *Design control:* A publisher rarely offers the writer any say
  about the design of the cover or interior of the book. Publishers may even change the title. The first indication of what
  the book will look like comes when the writer is sent a

photocopy of the cover and galleys of the text. This can be frightening. I know a professional writer who wrote a non-fiction book about his experiences in the United States Marine Corps and sold it to a small press. The cover of this macho book was done in a dainty powder blue. Self-published authors don't take this risk.

- *Money:* With traditional publishers, the writer is usually given approximately 10 percent of the book's retail cover price. In some cases it's 7 to 10 percent of the *wholesale* price (anywhere from 40 to 50 percent off the cover price). If a self-published book has a built-in marketplace and can sell 5,000 copies, the author could make 20 to 30 percent of the retail price.

- *Distribution:* Publishers print most new books in small lots, perhaps 5,000 copies. All too often those 5,000 copies are distributed, left in book stores for one month, then remaindered (sold for 10 to 25 cents a copy to wholesale distributors). If the publisher doesn't promote the book, the odds of its making the bestseller charts are dismal.

    Writer Calvin Trillin once wrote, "I conducted a study (using my usual controls) that showed the average shelf-life of a trade book to be somewhere between milk and yogurt. It is true that some books by Harold Robbins or any member of the Irving Wallace family last longer on the shelves, but they contain preservatives."

    With a self-published book the writer will certainly take an active interest in selling, promoting and "preserving" it.

- *Reprint:* If your independently published book does well in the marketplace, it can be sold as a reprint to a publishing house.

Of course, there are certain *disadvantages* to self-publishing as well.

- *Cost of publishing.* Depending on the number of copies printed, the cost of designing and printing a book can be excessive. The author has to be prepared to invest a certain amount of money to get the book published, and may not be able to recoup those expenses.

- *Distribution*. Although there are distribution companies that handle independently published books, there is no guarantee the distributor will promote or catalog your book for other than a short time.

Publishing a book boils down to caring. If you care enough about your idea and want others to read and enjoy what you have to say, you will find a place to sell and market your book—whether it be through traditional routes or independently.

Your book may never reach the sales levels of Dr. Spock's *Baby and Child Care*, but then, again—it might!

Write On

Fame is a bee
It has a song—
It has a sting—
Ah, too, it has a wing.

—Emily Dickinson

"Oh, I read your magazine article."

"Yes . . ." You tentatively say to your friend—and begin to feel wonderful inside.

"I loved it!"

The feeling is now one of joy.

"You know," your friend continues, "I've always wanted to be a writer. You know, like you, and have something published. Must be hard work, huh? *All those words*."

Yes, all those words. And you mastered them. You are no longer a fledgling writer, an aspiring writer. You are a *real* writer.

It's a great feeling.

Bibliography

"A Get-Started Bibliography for the Writer's Bookshelf"

Every writer should build and maintain a library of reference materials. Books that cannot be bought by the writer are available at the library.

1. Basic Grammar and Reference

Dictionary

Thesaurus

Elements of Style. E. B. White and William Strunk, Jr. (Macmillan Co., New York, 1959). Required reading for all writers. No exceptions.

A Manual for Writers. Kate L. Turabian (University of Chicago Press, Chicago and London, 1989). One of many English grammar manuals.

Write Right. Jan Venolia (Ten Speed Press, Berkeley, California, 1989). A good digest of punctuation, grammar and style.

The Transitive Vampire: A Handful of Grammar for the Innocent, the Eager, and the Doomed. Karen Elizabeth Gordon (Times Books, division of Random House, New York, 1989). The most entertaining (and weird) grammatical examples in print.

The Address Book: How to Reach Anyone Who Is Anyone. Michael

Levine, ed. (Perigee Books, Putnam, New York, 1984). Great
book for interviewers.

Tools of the Trade. Compiled by The American Society of Journalists and Authors Staff. (HarperCollins, New York, 1990).
Everything from office supplies to office design, from copiers to
computers.

Finding Facts Fast. Alden Todd (Ten Speed Press, Berkeley, California, 1989). Excellent insights on library research methods
and techniques.

The New York Times Guide to Reference Materials. Mona Mc-
Cormick (New American Library, New Jersey, 1989). Excellent
advice on finding research materials.

2. Markets

Writer's Market. Writer's Digest Books (Cincinnati, Ohio). An annual publication that lists 4,000 places to sell articles and books.

Writer's Handbook. Sylvia K. Burack, ed. (The Writer Inc.,
Boston). An annual publication listing 2,200 markets. Includes
100 chapters on how to write and sell writing.

The Writer and *Writer's Digest* magazines have monthly listings on
new or active article markets.

Not all books and journals can sit on your writer's bookshelf.
Certain research publications are available at your library.

3. Library Publications

The Reader's Guide to Periodical Literature. Listing of subject matter that has been written about in major magazines and journals.

Books in Print. A list of books available by subject, title and author.

Magazine Index. List of articles published in popular magazines.

UPI News. Listings by subject in today's newspapers.

Newsearch and *National Newspaper Index*. Listing of subjects in
major newspapers.

Literary Market Place (LMP). An annual publication listing agents, book publishers and magazine editors.

International Directory of Little Magazines and Small Presses. Published annually by Dustbooks, Paradise, California.

ADDITIONAL RESOURCE PUBLICATIONS:

The AMS Ayer Directory of Publications
Ulrich's International Periodicals
The Gale Directory of Publications
The Standard Periodical Directory

4. Publications from the Government

Selected U.S. Government Publications. A monthly catalogue of pamphlets.

The United States Government Manual. Information on all government branches.

Index

_____

_____

_____

_____

_____

_____

I n d e x

ABOUT THE AUTHOR

A retired navy aircraft carrier pilot, Cork Millner writes theatrical plays, wine books, travel pieces, and celebrity profiles. He has interviewed such famous people as Jimmy Stewart, Jonathan Winters, Julia Child, Jane Seymour, Rod Steiger, Bo Derek, and Steve Martin. He has written eleven books, including another one for writers, *The Art of Interviewing*. Cork lives in Santa Barbara, California.